WORDS UNDE

Also by Naomi Shihab Nye

Different Ways to Pray
Hugging the Jukebox
Yellow Glove
Mint (a chapbook of paragraphs)
This Same Sky (editor)
Sitti's Secrets (a picture book for children)
Red Suitcase
Benito's Dream Bottle (a picture book)
The Tree is Older Than You Are: A Bilingual Gathering
of Poems and Stories from Mexico (editor)
I Feel a Little Jumpy Around You (co-editor with Paul B. Janeczko)
Never in a Hurry (essays)
Lullaby Raft (a picture book)
Habibi (a novel for teenagers)
The Space Between Our Footsteps: Poems and Paintings from
the Middle East (editor)

WORDS UNDER THE WORDS
Selected Poems

Naomi Shihab Nye

The Eighth Mountain Press
A Far Corner Book
Portland, Oregon
1995

The poems in this book are selected from *Hugging the Jukebox* (originally published by E.P. Dutton, reprinted by Breitenbush Books), *Different Ways to Pray*, and *Yellow Glove* (both published by Breitenbush Books). The author is grateful to the editors of the publications in which many of these poems first appeared.

"Nothin' " copyright © 1971 by Townes Van Zandt, used by permission of Jeanene Van Zandt, Silver Dollar Music Publishing.

Library of Congress Cataloging-in-Publication Data
Nye, Naomi Shihab.
    [Poems. Selections]
    Words under the words : selected poems / Naomi Shihab Nye.
        p.   cm.
    "A Far Corner book."
    ISBN 0-933377-32-0 (hardcover) -- ISBN 0-933377-29-0
(paperback)
    I. Title.
PS3564.Y44A6 1995
811' .54--dc20   94-43072

Distributed to the trade by Consortium Book Sales & Distribution

Far Corner Books thanks Ruth Gundle and Brian Booth for their support and encouragement.

Far Corner Books
3844 S.W. Jerald Way
Portland, Oregon 97221

FIRST EDITION
9

With ongoing gratitude,
in memory of William Stafford.

The day I found his poems was a lucky day.
And every day thereafter.

Contents

from Hugging the Jukebox

from Yellow Glove

Loose Leaf

I was thumbing through a childhood picture album, its vintage red cover embossed with the golden word PHOTOGRAPHS, wondering exactly when and how all the pages let go of one another. They were still stacked, but no longer chronological or bound at the seam. I used to dream of having a loose-leaf life (as opposed to a spiral notebook kind of life) and guessed those old black and white photographs must have heard me.

Here I am wearing a polka-dotted headscarf, soberly pushing a stuffed rabbit in a baby carriage. Preparing to blow out two candles on a cake. Holding and being held. With neighbors who disappeared into the world and were never seen by us again. With baby brother freshly home from the hospital. With grandparents who died. With the cat that froze in the snow one winter. We tried to thaw him out in a warm oven. The underpants, the shutters, the wooden bedframes, the plump 1950s sofas. Here are the friendly immigrants who frequented our address and the concrete steps everybody fell down and the trees that may or may not still be rooted in the deep, silent ground. I wore a party dress and stood grinning with my legs crossed like an X. Immediately after that picture was taken, I fell over and hit my head on the fence. It was the first time I realized how quickly a day could change.

I think of the invisible pictures between the pictures, and under them. What was said that made us all look that way at just that moment? The gleam of particulars. My life, anybody's life. I've looked at albums belonging to people I barely know and could swear I recognized people in their photographs. Isn't that what happens with poems? When we let that luckiness come in.

In one scene my sleek-skinned shirtless father and I are digging in a garden with pitchforks. Our soil looks lumpy and dry, clotted with weeds and grass. Behind us our neighbor's tomatoes stand neatly tied to poles, head-high. We must have been slow that year. "What did we ever plant?" my father asks, forty springs later, staring hard at the photograph.

"Tomatoes," I say. "We must have planted tomatoes too. Let's ask Mom. She'll remember."

The mystery of remembering has added its own light to the garden. Whatever existed then has deepened, been forgotten or restored in some other form. We planted our voices. We planted the things we feared and hoped they'd go away. We ourselves were going away, but each day felt like a whole world, rich and round and thick with dreams. Where are all those days no one took a picture of? Maybe they're in your album.

Different Ways to Pray

Negotiations with a Volcano

We will call you "Agua" like the rivers and cool jugs.
We will persuade the clouds to nestle around your neck
so you may sleep late.
We would be happy if you slept forever.
We will tend the slopes we plant, singing the songs
our grandfathers taught us before we inherited their fear.
We will try not to argue among ourselves.
When the widow demands extra flour, we will provide it,
remembering the smell of incense on the day of our Lord.

Please think of us as we are, tiny, with skins that burn easily.
Please notice how we have watered the shrubs around our houses
and transplanted the peppers into neat tin cans.
Forgive any anger we feel toward the earth,
when the rains do not come, or they come too much,
and swallow our corn.
It is not easy to be this small and live in your shadow.

Often while we are eating our evening meal
you cross our rooms like a thief,
touching first the radio and then the loom.
Later our dreams begin catching fire around the edges,
they burn like paper, we wake with our hands full of ash.

How can we live like this?
We need to wake and find our shelves intact,
our children slumbering in their quilts.
We need dreams the shape of lakes,
with mornings in them thick as fish.
Shade us while we cast and hook—
but nothing else, nothing else.

3

The Indian in the Kitchen

Her face is Central America—
from the edges, oceans stretch out.
Quietly, quietly, the years have left her,
traveling by ship.

To this one I would say, Tell me the story
you have not told anyone,
the tale braided into your skull and tied with a string.
Describe the sky on the night you wandered out into the village,
calling for your father who left Huehuetenango
and never returned.
The shift in your mother's eyes—
how suddenly there was a rock ledge no one could climb.
Tell me of the brothers dancing with piglets
the day before they were sold
or the nights the goats were restless in their pens
and the rooster crowed at the wrong hour,
before Volcan Fuego spit hot sand into the air.
My hands would learn the colors your hands know,
blue and purple, threaded together on the loom.
How you weave the ducks and frogs
so they line up end-to-end across the cloth.

Listen, no one introduces us,
yet all evening it is you I am visiting.
When you bring the tea, limes neatly arranged on a saucer,
I try to catch you, the brown valleys of your eyes,
so you would know that I am watching, listening,
I hear you dry the plates.
Always your gaze misses me,
you are looking somewhere else,
the couch, the wall,
as if you believe what the days have told you.

The days—small coins given in exchange
for an egg, a broom.
The days which say you are a simple woman,
there is no story larger than the mashed black bean,
the bird's clean cage.

Remembered

He wanted to be remembered so he gave people things
they would remember him by. A large trunk, handmade of
ash and cedar. A tool box with initials shaped of scraps.
A tea kettle that would sing every morning,
antique glass jars to fill with crackers, noodles, beans.
A whole family of jams he made himself from the figs and berries
that purpled his land.

He gave these things unexpectedly. You went to see him
and came home loaded. You said "Thank you" till your lips
grew heavy with gratitude and swelled shut.
Walking with him across the acres of piney forest,
you noticed the way he talked to everything, a puddle, a stump,
the same way he talked to you.
"I declare you do look purty sittin' there in that field
reflectin' the light like some kind of mirror, you know what?"
As if objects could listen.
As if earth had a memory too.

At night we propped our feet by the fireplace
and laughed and showed photographs and the fire remembered
all the crackling music it knew. The night remembered
how to be dark and the forest remembered how to be mysterious
and in bed, the quilts remembered how to tuck up under our chins.
Sleeping in that house was like falling down a deep well,
rocking in a bucket all night long.

In the mornings we'd stagger away from an unforgettable breakfast
of biscuits—he'd lead us into the next room
ready to show us something or curl another story into our ear.
He scrawled the episodes out in elaborate longhand
and gave them to a farmer's wife to type.

Stories about a little boy and a grandfather,
chickens and prayer tents, butter beans and lightning.
He was the little boy.
Some days his brain could travel backwards easier than it could
sit in a chair, right there.

When we left he'd say "Don't forget me! You won't forget me now,
will you?" as if our remembering could lengthen his life.
I wanted to assure him, there will always be a cabin in our blood
only you live in. But the need for remembrance silenced me,
a ringing rising up out of the soil's centuries, the ones
who plowed this land, whose names we do not know.

The Whole Self

"You put your whole self in
You put your whole self out
Whole self in and you shake it all about"
                    The Hokey Pokey

When I think of the long history of the self
on its journey to becoming the whole self, I get tired.
It was the kind of trip you keep making,

Over and over again, the bag you pack and repack so often
the shirts start folding themselves the minute
you take them off.

I kept detailed notes in a brown notebook. I could tell you
when the arm joined, when it fell off again,
when the heart found the intended socket and settled down to pumping.

I could make a map of lost organs, the scrambled liver,
the misplaced brain. Finally finally we met up with one another
on a street corner, in October, during the noon rush.

I could tell you what I was wearing. How suddenly
the face of the harried waitress *made sense*. I gave my order
in a new voice. Spoke the word *vegetables* like a precious code.

Had one relapse at a cowboy dance in Bandera, Texas,
under a sky so fat the full moon
was sitting right on top of us.

Give me back my villages, I moaned,
the ability to touch and remove the hand
without losing anything.

Take me off this mountain where six counties are visible at once.
I want to remember what it felt like, loving by inches.
You put in the whole self—I'll keep with the toe.

But no, it was like telling the eye not to blink.
The self held on to its perimeters, committed forever,
as if the reunion could not be reversed.

I jumped inside the ring, all of me. Dance, then, and I danced,
till the room blurred like water, like blood, *dance*,
and I was leaning headlong into the universe,

Dance! The whole self was a current, a fragile cargo,
a raft someone was paddling through the jungle,
and I was there, waving, and I would be there at the other end.

Minnows

All night I stare into the mirror
at the deep wrinkle beginning to show
on my forehead above the right eye.

I move the muscles of my face
to see where it comes from
and it comes from everywhere,
pain, joy, the look of being puzzled
and raising one eyebrow,
from the way I say YES too much,
I say YES when I mean NO
and the wrinkle grows.

It is cutting a line across my head
like a crack in a creek bottom—
starting small, shiver between two stones,
it ends up splitting the bed.

I wade carefully, feeling with feet—
smooth-skinned pebbles,
the minnow's effortless glide.

Eye-to-Eye

Please forgive this interruption.
I am forging a career,
a delicate enterprise
of eyes. Yours included.
We will meet at the corner,
you with your sack lunch,
me with my guitar.
We will be wearing our famous street faces,
anonymous as trees.
Suddenly you will see me,
you will blink, hesitant,
then realize I have not looked away.
For one brave second
we will stare
openly
from borderless skins.
This is my salary.
There are no days off.

The Dream

Sometimes a dream lands so hard
it flattens you.

I liked it better before, you moan,
waving my dream like a silk handkerchief,
light and soundless above my head.

It could have been anything,
a kite, a bird, a large balloon
with three passengers.

Instead, it landed in your lap,
you asked for it,
secretly you had been reeling it in for months
like a trapped fish.

Too big for the net—
it loves you more than you love it.

It wants to stay here forever,
smiling and cuddling
in the bosom of your days.

Grandfather's Heaven

My grandfather told me I had a choice.
Up or down, he said. Up or down.
He never mentioned east or west.

Grandpa stacked newspapers on his bed
and read them years after the news was relevant.
He even checked the weather reports.

Grandma was afraid of Grandpa
for some reason I never understood.
She tiptoed while he snored, rarely disagreed.

I liked Grandma because she gave me cookies
and let me listen to the ocean in her shell.
Grandma liked me even though my daddy was a Moslem.

I think Grandpa liked me too
though he wasn't sure what to do with it.
Just before he died, he wrote me a letter.

"I hear you're studying religion," he said.
"That's how people get confused.
Keep it simple. Down or up."

The Little Brother Poem

I keep seeing your car in the streets
but it never turns at our corner. I keep finding
little pieces of junk you saved, a packing box, a white rag,
and stashed in the shed for future uses. Today I am cleaning
the house. I take your old camping jug, poke my finger
through the rusted hole in the bottom, stack it on the trash
wondering if you'd yell at me, if you had other plans for it.

Little brother, when you were born I was glad. Believe this.
There is much you never forgave me for but I tell you now,
I wanted you.

It's true there are things I would change. Your face bleeding
the day you followed me and I pushed you in front of a bicycle.
For weeks your eyes hard on me under the bandages. For years
you quoted me back to myself, mean things I'd said that I didn't
remember. Last summer you disappeared into the streets of Dallas
at midnight on foot crying and I realized you'd been serious,
some strange bruise you still carried under the skin.

You're not little anymore. You passed me up and kept reminding me
I'd stopped growing. We're different, always have been,
you're Wall Street and I'm the local fruit market,
you're Pierre Cardin and I'm a used bandanna.
That's fine, I'll take differences over things that match.

If you were here today we wouldn't say this.
You'd be outside cranking up the lawnmower.
I'd be in here answering mail.
You'd pass through the house and say "You're a big help"
and I'd say "Don't mention it" and the door would close.

I think of the rest of our lives. You're on the edge of yours today.
Long-distance I said "Are you happy?" and your voice wasn't sure.
It sounded small, younger, it sounded like the little brother

I don't have anymore, the one who ran miniature trucks up my arms
telling me I was a highway, the one who believed me
when I told him monkeys arrived in the night to kidnap boys
with brown hair. I'm sorry for everything I did that hurt.
It's a large order I know, dumping out a whole drawer at once,
fingering receipts and stubs, trying to put them back
in some kind of shape so you'll be able to find everything later,
when you need it, and you don't have so much time.

Madison Street

Smoke from the chimney on the next roof

A chicken loose in the street
I carry it to the man next door who chops the wood
and he strokes its orange head

Wife protests   don't put that chicken in this yard
but he is already tearing the bread into tiny squares

I want to remember everything   the plump gray doves
lining up under the eaves   the way I sat at my desk all day
and the grandmother passed with her shopping cart
and the grandfather passed with his basket of clothes

The street a hundred years old   I tell myself
I am young   I was not here when all this started
still there is some larger belonging   leaves falling
I could have planted those trees

The World in Translation

It was a long climb out of the soil.
She counted off whole continents
as she lifted each foot,
imagined her dark years falling away like husks.
Soon she could feel objects come to life
in her hand, the peel of banana,
a lightly waxed pepper,
she accepted these into her home,
placed them in bowls where they could be watched.
There was nothing obscure about melons,
nothing involved about yams.
If she were to have anything to do with the world,
these would be her translators,
through these she would learn secrets of dying,
how to do it gracefully as the peach,
softening in silence,
or the mango, finely tuned to its own skin.

Different Ways to Pray

There was the method of kneeling,
a fine method, if you lived in a country
where stones were smooth.
The women dreamed wistfully of bleached courtyards,
hidden corners where knee fit rock.
Their prayers were weathered rib bones,
small calcium words uttered in sequence,
as if this shedding of syllables could somehow
fuse them to the sky.

There were the men who had been shepherds so long
they walked like sheep.
Under the olive trees, they raised their arms—
Hear us! We have pain on earth!
We have so much pain there is no place to store it!
But the olives bobbed peacefully
in fragrant buckets of vinegar and thyme.
At night the men ate heartily, flat bread and white cheese,
and were happy in spite of the pain,
because there was also happiness.

Some prized the pilgrimage,
wrapping themselves in new white linen
to ride buses across miles of vacant sand.
When they arrived at Mecca
they would circle the holy places,
on foot, many times,
they would bend to kiss the earth
and return, their lean faces housing mystery.

While for certain cousins and grandmothers
the pilgrimage occurred daily,
lugging water from the spring
or balancing the baskets of grapes.

These were the ones present at births,
humming quietly to perspiring mothers.
The ones stitching intricate needlework into children's dresses,
forgetting how easily children soil clothes.

There were those who didn't care about praying.
The young ones. The ones who had been to America.
They told the old ones, you are wasting your time.
      Time?—The old ones prayed for the young ones.
They prayed for Allah to mend their brains,
for the twig, the round moon,
to speak suddenly in a commanding tone.

And occasionally there would be one
who did none of this,
the old man Fowzi, for example, Fowzi the fool,
who beat everyone at dominoes,
insisted he spoke with God as he spoke with goats,
and was famous for his laugh.

My Father and the Figtree

For other fruits my father was indifferent.
He'd point at the cherry trees and say,
"See those? I wish they were figs."
In the evenings he sat by my bed
weaving folktales like vivid little scarves.
They always involved a figtree.
Even when it didn't fit, he'd stick it in.
Once Joha was walking down the road and he saw a figtree.
Or, he tied his camel to a figtree and went to sleep.
Or, later when they caught and arrested him,
his pockets were full of figs.

At age six I ate a dried fig and shrugged.
"That's not what I'm talking about!" he said,
"I'm talking about a fig straight from the earth—
gift of Allah!—on a branch so heavy it touches the ground.
I'm talking about picking the largest fattest sweetest fig
in the world and putting it in my mouth."
(Here he'd stop and close his eyes.)

Years passed, we lived in many houses, none had figtrees.
We had lima beans, zucchini, parsley, beets.
"Plant one!" my mother said, but my father never did.
He tended garden half-heartedly, forgot to water,
let the okra get too big.
"What a dreamer he is. Look how many things he starts
and doesn't finish."

The last time he moved, I got a phone call.
My father, in Arabic, chanting a song I'd never heard.
"What's that?"
"Wait till you see!"

He took me out to the new yard.
There, in the middle of Dallas, Texas,
a tree with the largest, fattest, sweetest figs in the world.
"It's a figtree song!" he said,
plucking his fruits like ripe tokens,
emblems, assurance
of a world that was always his own.

You Know Who You Are

Why do your poems comfort me, I ask myself.
Because they are upright, like straight-backed chairs.
I can sit in them and study the world as if it too
were simple and upright.

Because sometimes I live in a hurricane of words
and not one of them can save me.
Your poems come in like a raft, logs tied together,
they float.
I want to tell you about the afternoon
I floated on your poems
all the way from Durango Street to Broadway.

Fathers were paddling on the river with their small sons.
Three Mexican boys chased each other outside the library.
Everyone seemed to have some task, some occupation,
while I wandered uselessly in the streets I claim to love.

Suddenly I felt the precise body of your poems beneath me,
like a raft, I felt words as something portable again,
a cup, a newspaper, a pin.
Everything happening had a light around it,
not the light of Catholic miracles,
the blunt light of a Saturday afternoon.
Light in a world that rushes forward with us or without us.
I wanted to stop and gather up the blocks behind me
in this light, but it doesn't work.
You keep walking, lifting one foot, then the other,
saying "This is what I need to remember"
and then hoping you can.

Arriving at a Fish

It was the air which entered you,
drifting in the small boat.
The stories, the jokes, air swallowed them,
they became element, air and water,
an intercourse of branch and vine.
You arrived at the old muddy anchor in your sleep.
And you realized your allegiance to fishing
had nothing to do with fish, or little, anyway,
so when the great bass came writhing out of the water
you were shocked.
He lay in the bottom of the boat,
a sudden silver word.
His mouth was angry, his mouth was an old man
missing a bus.
You touched the scales, the flapping fins and sharp tail,
with a hesitant welcome.
And later it was you and it was not you
who carried the bass on the strong yellow line
and showed him to the neighbors,
a photo snapped in a bright room.
Inside, your own gills were opening and closing
like remnants of an early life,
when this hadn't happened yet
and you were traveling through water,
dodging anything that suggested an end.

Long Distance

for my mother

Your voice crackles, sleet on the wire.
Days now, we wake in fevers, our limbs speak
garbled languages of ache and flush.

"I've been having my vision of infinity," you say.
When I ask what it looks like, you pause.
You have never trusted words.

From other conversations, sound seeps through,
a woman's question, a man's laugh.
I picture you cupping the phone in your hands.

"Tell me. Is it good?"
But you aren't sure. Perhaps a golden weightlessness,
rising and rising. This is what I would like to believe,
trapped in my heavy layers of flannel and socks.

Perhaps something else, something deep and falling.
Tell me where you go in these silences
and I will say if I have been there.

I remember, as a child, "The World's Highest Suspension Bridge,"
and our timid steps, walking out a little way,
clinging to the rail.
Since then I have met a man who fell from a high building,
because he wanted to, because he dreamed of falling
till it was the only thing he could do.
He lived to tell reporters it didn't hurt as much as
falling from a standing position or skinning a knee.
Now he wears moccasins without soles,
he moves quietly from room to room.
I have followed him, Mother, and I found out
he doesn't know more than I do, or you, or any of us.

I had a vision of infinity I never told you about.
I was ten, on our trip to the farm—a sow was in labor.
You were all keeping vigil in the barn.
By myself I walked back to the house. A television was on,
no one watching it, just on.
I sat on the couch. For a moment between programs
the screen swirled an outer-space landscape,
stars and galaxies, dazzling miracles of light.
Suddenly something dropped—
it was the first moment I knew I would die.
I would not always be healthy, brown,
breathing easily inside my skin.
And then I fell farther, I lost my name, the month,
I traveled deeper than I had ever gone,
back behind the point where I began,
before I became someone knowing herself as someone.
I became that endless black beyond the stars,
knowing nothing, not knowing what it had not known,
and realized it was where I was going,
just as it was where I had been.
For seconds, Mother, or maybe minutes,
I was no longer your child or anything human
and then the screen changed and Walt Disney took over
and I switched it off and wandered out into the dark.

Listen, did you recognize me later, in the barn,
kneeling over the squealing pigs?
If so, tell me now, as I have told you,
how far you journey, how strange it is to come back.

Biography of an Armenian Schoolgirl

I have lived in the room of stone where voices become
bones buried under us long ago. Where you could dig
for centuries uncovering the same sweet dust.

My hands dream crescent-shaped cakes,
trapped moons on a narrow veined earth.
All day I am studying my hands—I am giving them new things to hold.

Travel, I say. They become boats.
Go—the bird squirms to detach from the arm.
Across the courtyards, a radio rises up and explodes.

What is the history of Europe to us if we cannot choose our own husbands?
Yesterday my father met with the widower, the man with no hair.
How will I sleep with him, I who have never slept away from my mother?

Once I bought bread from the vendor with the humped back.
I carried it home singing, I thought the days had doors in them
that would swing open in front of me.

Now I copy the alphabets of three languages,
imagining the loops in my Arabic letters are eyes.
What you do when you are tired of what you see,

what happens to the gray body when it is laid in the earth,
these are the subjects which concern me. But they teach algebra.
They pull our hair back and examine our nails.

Every afternoon, predictable passage of sun across a wall.
I would fly out of here. Travel, I say.
I would go so far away my life would be a small thing behind me.

They teach physics, chemistry. I throw my book out the window,
watch the pages scatter like wings.
I stitch the professor's jacket to the back of his chair.

There is something else we were born for.
I almost remember it. While I write, a ghost writes on the same tablet,
achieves a different sum.

Kansas

Driving across the center of Kansas
at midnight, we're talking about
all our regrets, the ones we didn't marry,
who married each other, who aren't happy,
who should have married us.
Ah, it's a tough world, you say,
taking the wrong road.
Signposts appear and vanish, ghostly,
ALTERNATE 74.
I'm not aware it's the wrong road,
I don't live here,
this is the flattest night in the world
and I just arrived.
Grain elevators startle us,
dark monuments
rimmed by light.
Later you pull over
and put your head on the wheel.
I'm lost, you moan. I have no idea where we are.
I pat your arm.
It's alright, I say.
Surely there's a turn-off up here somewhere.
My voice amazes me,
coming out of the silence,
a lit spoon,
here,
swallow this.

The Art of Disappearing

When they say Don't I know you?
say no.

When they invite you to the party
remember what parties are like
before answering.
Someone telling you in a loud voice
they once wrote a poem.
Greasy sausage balls on a paper plate.
Then reply.

If they say We should get together
say why?

It's not that you don't love them anymore.
You're trying to remember something
too important to forget.
Trees. The monastery bell at twilight.
Tell them you have a new project.
It will never be finished.

When someone recognizes you in a grocery store
nod briefly and become a cabbage.
When someone you haven't seen in ten years
appears at the door,
don't start singing him all your new songs.
You will never catch up.

Walk around feeling like a leaf.
Know you could tumble any second.
Then decide what to do with your time.

At Otto's Place

for Rubina and Otto Schroeder

There is a therapy in fields—
east, west, nothing speaks but the sky.
Jackrabbit crouches in a gully,
ears poised, ready to spring.
Cattle raise their heads—they are listeners,
as I become the deepest listener
where there is least to hear.

Somehow my limbs begin returning,
fingers form again at the ends of my arms.
On the earth, feet receive direct knowledge—
hiking the rise by the fish-tank,
the tangled path between the barns,
they step and climb, alive.

How is it, such wealthy redemption
in a fence post, a rusting stove?
Far away a coyote chants.
It is wonderful to think we will never meet.
Going home later, thirty deer will cross single file
in our headlights, followed by a pack of grunting pigs.

Could I live like this? I ask myself
and I know, somehow, I must.
More and more my life is peeling paint,
straight horizons.
More and more my name dissolves in the air,
salt, something invisible I taste,
and forget.

Ring around the moon—tomorrow, rain.
But tonight the stars are up.

We sit on the steps with flashlights,
picking out animals in the fields,
picking them out, briefly,
then giving them back their dark.

And if the world remembers us,
it is not that we have done anything,
but more, that we have witnessed
the cistern's quiet bucket
and for awhile tonight,
dropped it down.

The Music Box

I don't know who gave me this instrument,
what happened to the box that once housed
this now-bare motor . . . I turn the knob,
again, again, till the thing is tightly wound,
then watch the intricate wheels spin against one another
clicking out tiny metallic notes.
It is a familiar song but I couldn't name it.
It repeats over and over, a miniature anthem
vibrating in my hand.
I feel there is something I should remember,
at least who gave it to me, but this memory has fallen away
like so many others. Sometimes I feel the mind's
thin shavings scattering the minute they fall,
like the notes of this music-box disappearing into Monday,
even the ones that play together, the highest note,
even the pause.

For Mohammed on the Mountain

1.
Uncle Mohammed, you mystery, you distant faceless face,
lately you travel across the ocean and tap me on my shoulder
and say "See?" And I think I know what you are talking about,
though we have never talked, though you have never traveled anywhere
in twenty-five years, or at least, anywhere anyone knows about.
Since my childhood, you were the one I cared for,
you of all the uncles, the elder brother of the family.
I'd pump my father—"But why did he go to the mountain?
What happened to him?" and my father, in his usual quiet way,
would shrug and say—"Who knows?"
All I knew was you packed up, you moved to the mountain,
you would not come down.
This fascinated me: How does he get food? Who does he talk to?
What does he do all day?
In grade school my friends had uncles who rode motorcycles,
who cooked steaks outdoors or paid for movies.
I preferred you, in all your silence.
In my mind you were like a god, living close to clouds,
fearless and strong, with no one to sing you to sleep.
And I wanted to know you, to touch hands, to have you look at me
and recognize your blood, a small offspring
who did not find you in the least bit
nuts.

2.
I wonder how much news you know. That Naomi, your sister
for whom I was partially named, is dead.
That one brother shot himself "by mistake"—
that your brothers Izzat and Mufli have twenty-two children
already marrying each other.
That my father edits one of the largest newspapers in America
but keeps an Arabic inscription above his door, *Ahlan Wa Sahlan,*
a door you will never enter.

We came to your country, Uncle, we lived there a year
among sheep and stones, camels and fragrant oils,
and you would not come down to see us.
I think that hurt my father, though he never said so.
It hurt me, scanning the mountains for sight of your hut,
quizzing the relatives and learning nothing.
Are you angry with us? Do you think my father forgot you
when he packed his satchel and boarded the ship?
Believe me, Uncle, my father is closer to you
than the brothers who never left. When he tends plants,
he walks slowly. His steps sing of the hills.
And when he stirs the thick coffee and grinds the cardamom seed
you think he feels like an American?
You think he forgets the call to prayer?

Oh Uncle, forgive me, how long is your beard?

3.
Maybe you had other reasons.
Maybe you didn't go up the mountain because you were angry.
This is what I am learning, the voice I hear when I wake at 3 a.m.
It says, Teach me how little I need to live
and I can't tell if it is me talking, or you,
or the walls of the room. How little, how little,
and the world jokes and says, how much.
Money, events, ambitions, plans, oh Uncle,
I have made myself a quiet place in the swirl.
I think you would like it.
Yesterday I learned how many shavings of wood the knife discards
to leave one smoothly whittled spoon.
Today I read angles of light through the window,
first they touch the floor, then the bed,
till everything is luminous, curtains flung wide.
As for friends, they are fewer and dearer,
and the ones who remain seem also to be climbing mountains
in various ways, though we dream we will meet at the top.
Will you be there?
Gazing out over valleys and olive orchards,
telling us sit, sit,
you expected us all along.

The Words Under the Words

for Sitti Khadra, north of Jerusalem

My grandmother's hands recognize grapes,
the damp shine of a goat's new skin.
When I was sick they followed me,
I woke from the long fever to find them
covering my head like cool prayers.

My grandmother's days are made of bread,
a round pat-pat and the slow baking.
She waits by the oven watching a strange car
circle the streets. Maybe it holds her son,
lost to America. More often, tourists,
who kneel and weep at mysterious shrines.
She knows how often mail arrives,
how rarely there is a letter.
When one comes, she announces it, a miracle,
listening to it read again and again
in the dim evening light.

My grandmother's voice says nothing can surprise her.
Take her the shotgun wound and the crippled baby.
She knows the spaces we travel through,
the messages we cannot send—our voices are short
and would get lost on the journey.
Farewell to the husband's coat,
the ones she has loved and nourished,
who fly from her like seeds into a deep sky.
They will plant themselves. We will all die.

My grandmother's eyes say Allah is everywhere, even in death.
When she talks of the orchard and the new olive press,
when she tells the stories of Joha and his foolish wisdoms,
He is her first thought, what she really thinks of is His name.

"Answer, if you hear the words under the words—
otherwise it is just a world with a lot of rough edges,
difficult to get through, and our pockets full of stones."

White Silk

"Forget everything, stop doing anything, and try to rest completely.
Try to pass ten thousand years in one thought! Try to be the cold
ashes and the worn-out tree! Try to be a length of white silk."
                                        Zen Master Shih Shuang

I dreamed of white silk the night
you pointed a finger at me saying
there were caves in my history
I refused to explore. You had a clue, you said,
and would have led me down the damp passageways
swinging your lamp.
In my life, historically, that was the moment
you disappeared.

I dreamed of white silk on the last day of the year.
Crouched on my roof, I watched the neighborhood ignite,
quick bright fountains lighting up the trees.
I heard the distant yell of children,
the joy of an ending and a beginning with a name.
And I knew there were things I cared about
and things I did not care about
just as I knew the blunt sidewalks leading east and west.
The lifelong vocation of standing wherever you are
and knowing which way to walk next—
I dreamed the roof was white silk, folded carefully on a large bolt,
the center to which I would return and return.

I dreamed white silk on the day I realized
detail, that wealth we live by, is also
another method of execution.
I was carrying keys on a large silver ring—
trying to find the right key for a lock that would not budge,
with a time limit, someone needed in.

I felt myself juggling under a weight that said,
This too is the world.
For some, the only world.
I knew then why the faces of women behind counters are often
expressionless, why their eyes are coins
with only one side.

> On the day I realized I would be riding
> this slow pony forever
>
> On the day my mother's voice broke
> like a teacup in my hands
> and I saw us all standing on tiny islands
> off the coast of Alaska
> drifting up into cooler regions
> where the only relationship is ice and sky
>
> On the day we talked about life after death
> and I said, If there is none
> that doesn't change anything

In a small town, in a general store,
I saw a roll of white silk sleeping high on a shelf.
Storekeeper counting beans,
told me if I wanted anything, better get it,
he was closing out in auction the coming week.
I unrolled the silk. Smooth brown lines at every crease.
In the corner, his wife darned slips and winked at me.
"Don't believe it, honey.
You want anything—you take your time."

What People Do

November   November   November   the days crowd together
like families of leaves   in a dry field
I pick up a round stone   take it to my father
who lies in bed waiting for his heart to mend
and he turns it over and over in his hands

My father is writing me the story of his village
He tells what people did   in another country
before I was born   how his best friend was buried alive
and the boy survived two days in the ground
how my father was lowered into a well on ropes   to discover
clay jars a thousand years old   how each jar held seeds
carob and melon   and the villagers chose secrecy
knowing the British would come with trucks and dig up their town

My father's handwriting changes from page to page
sometimes wild scrawl and disconnected letters
sometimes a new serious upward slant

And me   I travel the old roads again and again
wearing a different life in a house surrounded by trees
At night the dropping pecans make little clicks above us
Doors closing

More and more I understand what people do
I appreciate the daily braveries   clean white shirts
morning greetings between old men

Again I see how   once the boat tips   you never forget
the sensation of drowning
even if you sing yourself the familiar songs

Today my face is stone   my eyes are buckets
I walk the streets lowering them into everything
but they come up empty

I would tell my father
    I cannot move one block without you
    I will never recover from your love
yet I stand by his bed saying things I have said before
and he answers   and we go on this way
smoothing the silences
nothing can heal

Kindness

Before you know what kindness really is
you must lose things,
feel the future dissolve in a moment
like salt in a weakened broth.
What you held in your hand,
what you counted and carefully saved,
all this must go so you know
how desolate the landscape can be
between the regions of kindness.
How you ride and ride
thinking the bus will never stop,
the passengers eating maize and chicken
will stare out the window forever.

Before you learn the tender gravity of kindness,
you must travel where the Indian in a white poncho
lies dead by the side of the road.
You must see how this could be you,
how he too was someone
who journeyed through the night with plans
and the simple breath that kept him alive.

Before you know kindness as the deepest thing inside,
you must know sorrow as the other deepest thing.
You must wake up with sorrow.
You must speak to it till your voice
catches the thread of all sorrows
and you see the size of the cloth.

Then it is only kindness that makes sense anymore,
only kindness that ties your shoes
and sends you out into the day to mail letters and purchase bread,

only kindness that raises its head
from the crowd of the world to say
It is I you have been looking for,
and then goes with you everywhere
like a shadow or a friend.

Colombia

Bolivia

All day we held on tight through dust
knowing the truck was taking us south
Lake Titicaca a blue slice on the left-hand side

An Indian sat on your feet so long
you said your whole body went numb
The book described the border town
with one accurate word
"miserable"

Crossing the border a hard wind was blowing us
back and back   your hair   your jacket
and we pushed forward   heads down   because night was coming
because all of Peru lay behind us and we needed another country
like hungry men need bread

We coughed our way through the streets
packs heavy on us   calling *Donde esta Bolivia?*
to the brown women perched on curbs
How odd it was to be walking like that
out of our lives   into our lives
the last few coins loose in the pocket
and no lights on the other side

Walking Down Blanco Road at Midnight

There is a folding into the self which occurs
when the lights are small on the horizon
and no light is shining into the face.

It happens in a quiet place.
It is a quiet folding,
like going to sleep in
the comfortable family home.
When everyone goes to sleep
the house folds up.
The windows shut their eyes.
If you are inside you are automatically folded.
If you are outside walking by the folded house
you feel so lonesome you think you are going crazy.

You are not going crazy.
You are beginning to fold up in your own single way.
You feel your edges move toward the center,
your heart like a folded blanket unfolding
and folding in with everything contained.
You feel you do not need anyone to love you anymore
because you already feel everything,
you feel it, you fold it, and for a while now,
it will quietly rest.

Adios

It is a good word, rolling off the tongue
no matter what language you were born with.
Use it. Learn where it begins,
the small alphabet of departure,
how long it takes to think of it,
then say it, then be heard.

Marry it. More than any golden ring,
it shines, it shines.
Wear it on every finger
till your hands dance,
touching everything easily,
letting everything, easily, go.

Strap it to your back like wings.
Or a kite-tail. The stream of air behind a jet.
If you are known for anything,
let it be the way you rise out of sight
when your work is finished.

Think of things that linger: leaves,
cartons and napkins, the damp smell of mold.

Think of things that disappear.

Think of what you love best,
what brings tears into your eyes.

Something that said *adios* to you
before you knew what it meant
or how long it was for.

Explain little, the word explains itself.
Later perhaps. Lessons following lessons,
like silence following sound.

Coming into Cuzco

"Being born is going blind and bowing down a thousand times."
Townes Van Zandt

We woke early and found the streets already crowded
with taxis, travelers, Indians loading yams.
At the airport we waited for the plane that would lift us
out of those mountains and I was a broken jug,
nothing could fill me. I wandered among the Europeans
in their new alpaca sweaters, thinking, everyone has a sweater,
this is Peru. You stood with hands sunk in your pockets,
your brown hat tipped back on your head.
How easily you joined the ticket line, how easily you mentioned coffee,
but I was watching a funeral, black-cloaked Indians
comforting an old man with white hair
who had just stepped off the plane followed by a casket.
I was listening to the herd of them wailing on the runway,
thinking the man in the center was the same shape as my father,
thinking, this is Peru, this is more than Peru.
I could not speak it. That morning my mouth was a buried spoon.
I wanted to throw my life down in front of me
and rear up straight like an animal before he gallops into the woods.
But the plane rose and we were riding it.
They gave us sugar candies because we were so high, so high.
I looked down on that land I was beginning to recognize
and wondered at all the grief I have not yet experienced,
how it would be to be riding next to the body of the one you have loved
on the day it no longer carries a breath, and I said to myself,
you know nothing, you are your own dead weight.

When we landed I was still dragging the sack of stones,
unable to joke or focus on the guidebook.
"Finding Your Way," it said, and I thought,
this will take more than a map.

We were riding a bus into the city.
A baby pressed among the passengers shouted *Vamos!* every time the bus
    paused.
Suddenly a laugh, a stranger, was sliding into my throat.
I thought how far we had come and finally we were coming into Cuzco.
A young girl pushed forward toward the door.
I saw the bright nosegay of flowers she guarded carefully.
Vamos! And she handed me one perfect pink rose,
because we had noticed each other, and that was all.
One rose coming into Cuzco and I was thinking
it should not be so difficult to be happy in this world.

Hugging the Jukebox

For Lost and Found Brothers

Where were you in winters of snow,
what ceiling did you stare at
before the dark came home to hold your hand?
What did your mama tell you about the world?

Facts interest me less than the trailing smoke of stories.
Where were you when no one else was there?

You lived in France at the foot of mountains
with paper, with creamy white days.
You hiked railroad tracks dreaming of mirrors,
how one life reflects another, goes back and back and back.
You stood in rooms, your black eyes birds barely landed,
and learned the long river that was your voice.
Thank you, a stone thrown in, a stone quietly sinking.
Thank you, a ripple returned.
So today when you bend to sign the first page of your book
there are other things to thank too,
the days folded behind you, in your wake,
this day connected, more mirrors, more birds.

For you, brothers.
For the blood rivers invisibly harbored.
For the grandfathers who murmured the same songs.
And for the ways we know each other years before meeting,
how strangely and suddenly, on the lonely porches,
in the sleepless mouth of the night,
the sadness drops away, we move forward,
confident we were born into a large family,
our brothers cover the earth.

Lights from Other Windows

Driving west tonight, the city dissolves behind us.
I keep feeling we're going farther than we're going,
a journey that started in the deep inkwell
out of which all our days are written.
Nothing is said to indicate a monument,
yet I perch on the edge of some new light.
The hills could crack open and a pointed beam,
like the beams on miners' hats, could pick us off this road.
Signals blinking, we arrive in a bright room
of greetings and hands. But when the stories spill,
I feel myself floating off alone into that night we just left,
that cool black bag of darkness, where black deer
nibbled invisible grasses and black fences divided one thing
from the next. A voice in my earliest ears *not this, not this*
and the lit windows of childhood rise up,
the windows of houses where strangers lived,
light slanting across black roads,
that light which said *what a small flicker is given
to each of us to know*. For seconds I dreamed their rooms
and tables, was comforted by promise of a billion other lives.
Like stars. Like knowing the Milky Way
is made of more stars than any naked eye can count.
Like having someplace to go when your glowing restlessness
lifts you out of rooms, becomes a wing,
takes you farther than you will have traveled
when your own life ends.

At the Seven-Mile Ranch, Comstock, Texas

I live like I know what I'm doing.

When I hand the horses a square of hay,
when I walk the road of stones
or chew on cactus pulp,
there's a drumming behind me,
the day opens up to let me pass through.

I know the truth,
how always I'm following each small sign that appears.
This sheep that materialized behind a clump of cenizo bushes
knows I didn't see him till he raised his head.

Out here it's impossible to be lonely.
The land walking beside you is your oldest friend,
pleasantly silent, like already you've told the best stories
and each of you knows how much the other made up.

Daily

These shriveled seeds we plant,
corn kernel, dried bean,
poke into loosened soil,
cover over with measured fingertips

These T-shirts we fold into
perfect white squares

These tortillas we slice and fry to crisp strips
This rich egg scrambled in a gray clay bowl

This bed whose covers I straighten
smoothing edges till blue quilt fits brown blanket
and nothing hangs out

This envelope I address
so the name balances like a cloud
in the center of the sky

This page I type and retype
This table I dust till the scarred wood shines
This bundle of clothes I wash and hang and wash again
like flags we share, a country so close
no one needs to name it

The days are nouns: touch them
The hands are churches that worship the world

The Lost Parrot

Carlos bites the end of his pencil
He's trying to write a dream-poem, but waves at me, frowning

     I had a parrot

He talks slowly, his voice travels far
to get out of his body

     A dream-parrot?
     No, a real parrot!
     Write about it

He squirms, looks nervous, everyone else is almost finished
and he hasn't started

     It left
     What left?
     The *parrot*

He hunches over the table, pencil gripped in fist,
shaping the heavy letters
Days later we will write story-poems, sound-poems,
but always the same subject for Carlos

     It left

He will insist on reading it and the class will look puzzled
The class is tired of the parrot

     Write more, Carlos
     I can't

     Why not?

     I don't know   where   it went

Each day when I leave he stares at the ceiling
Maybe he is planning an expedition
into the back streets of San Antonio
armed with nets and ripe mangoes
He will find the parrot nesting in a rain gutter
This time he will guard it carefully, make sure it stays

Before winter comes and his paper goes white
in all directions

Before anything else he loves
gets away

Where Children Live

Homes where children live exude a pleasant rumpledness,
like a bed made by a child, or a yard littered with balloons.

To be a child again one would need to shed details
till the heart found itself dressed in the coat with a hood.
Now the heart has taken on gloves and mufflers,
the heart never goes outside to find something to "do."
And the house takes on a new face, dignified.
No lost shoes blooming under bushes.
No chipped trucks in the drive.
Grown-ups like swings, leafy plants, slow-motion back and forth.
While the yard of a child is strewn with the corpses
of bottle-rockets and whistles,
anything whizzing and spectacular, brilliantly short-lived.

Trees in children's yards speak in clearer tongues.
Ants have more hope. Squirrels dance as well as hide.
The fence has a reason to be there, so children can go in and out.
Even when the children are at school, the yards glow
with the leftovers of their affection,
the roots of the tiniest grasses curl toward one another
like secret smiles.

Martita y Luisa

1.
Martita, a carriage of windows is passing by!

Aye, aye, little sister,
tomorrow they will all be closed.
You will sing me the song
of the folded bug.

Martita, the river is crayons,
the color blue will make me a boat!

And it will sink, little sparrow,
there are holes in the bottoms of boats
that are wider than our names. Even a name
like Martita.

2.
All day they spin marbles among stones.

Who is the street-sweeper?
Where does he sleep from morning till night?

He lives in a shadow room.
His mouth is the moon that is almost gone.

Where does the mailman put down his bag?

In the cemetery, on the grave of a child
who never learned to read or write.

Why does the Chinese woman
with a bandanna knotted on her head
push a cartload of cabbages
six miles every day?

They will wilt if she does not get there.

But where? Where is she going
in the sun, in the rain?

Now you come to the question made of ice.
It melts if I tell you.
Better to keep a few things floating,
a few things for the future,
little sister, your turn.

3.
A marble blue as a birthday sky
swallowed by grass.

You were born before me.
Does that mean you die first too?

At the hour when mothers scrabble in cupboards
tilting the jars of oil,
light falls down among trees
like an old washed sheet.
All night it will be drying
in the cracks where lives come together,
where things are lost and never claimed.
Each sister thinks the other has it
in her pocket. Goodnight little world
of lizards, as they brush the hair,
as they snap the gowns they will wear
into the other country, pulling each other
by long long hands.

West Side

In certain neighborhoods
the air is paved with names.
Domingo, Monico, Francisco,
shining rivulets of sound.
Names opening wet circles
inside the mouth,
sprinkling bright vowels
across the deserts of
Bill, Bob, John.

The names are worn
on silver linked chains.
Maria lives in Pablo Alley,
Esperanza rides the Santa Rosa bus!
They click together like charms.
O save us from the boarded-up windows,
the pistol crack in a dark backyard,
save us from the leaky roof,
the rattled textbook which never smiles.
Let the names be verses
in a city that sings!

For Rose on Magnolia Street

You ask me to remove my shoes
and it is correct somehow,
this stripping down in your presence.
Do you recognize in me
a bone, a window, a bell?

You are translating a child's poem
about the color gray.
I float through your rooms,
peeking at titles, fingering the laces
you drape from your walls.

The first place I visited you,
a tree grew out of your bedroom,
hole cut in the ceiling.
Today there are plants in your bathtub.
Their leaves are thick and damp.

I want to plant myself beside you
and soak up some of your light.
When the streetlamps cross their hands,
when the uncles shuffle home from the market
murmuring of weather and goats,
you lean into a delicate shawl,
the letters people write you
begin glowing in your baskets.
Yesterday you wrote of the dog-man
who wanders everywhere
followed by a pack of seven hounds.
Soon you will tell us the secret
behind our grandmothers' soft hair.

The Trashpickers, Madison Street

On the edge of dawn's pale eye,
the trashpickers are lifting the lid of every can,
poking inside with bent hanger and stick.
They murmur in a language soft as rags.
What have we here?
Their colorless overcoats drift and grow wings.

They pull a creaking wagon, tinfoil wads, knotted string,
to the cave where sacraments of usefulness are performed.
Kneel to the triple weddings of an old nail.
Rejoice in the rebirth of envelopes.
The crooked skillet finds its first kingdom
on a shelf where nothing is new.

They dream small dreams, furry ones,
a swatch of velvet passed hand-to-hand.
Their hearts are compasses fixed to the ground
and their love, more like moss than like fire.

Rebellion against the North Side

There will be no monograms on our skulls.
You who are training your daughters to check for the words
"Calvin Klein" before they look to see if there are pockets
are giving them no hands to put in those pockets.

You are giving them eyes that will find nothing solid in stones.
No comfort in rough land, nameless sheep trails.
No answers from things which do not speak.

Since when do children sketch dreams with price tags attached?
Don't tell me they were born this way.
We were all born like empty fields.
What we are now shows what has been planted.

Will you remind them there were people
who hemmed their days with thick-spun wool
and wore them till they fell apart?

Think of darkness hugging the houses,
caring nothing for the material of our pajamas.
Think of the delicate mesh of neckbones
when you clasp the golden chains.
These words the world rains back and forth
are temporary as clouds.
Clouds? Tell your children to look up.
The sky is the only store worth shopping in
for anything as long as a life.

The Song

From somewhere
a calm musical note arrives.
You balance it on your tongue,
a single ripe grape,
till your whole body glistens.
In the space between breaths
you apply it to any wound
and the wound heals.

Soon the nights will lengthen,
you will lean into the year
humming like a saw.
You will fill the lamps with kerosene,
knowing somewhere a line breaks,
a city goes black,
people dig for candles in the bottom drawer.
You will be ready. You will use the song like a match.
It will fill your rooms
opening rooms of its own
so you sing, I did not know
my house was this large.

The Passport Photo

"The Passport Office welcomes photographs which depict the
applicant as relaxed and smiling."
    Passport Application

Before they shoot, I think of where I am going,
Chile, the world's thinnest country,
the bright woven hats on the Indians of Peru.

I swallow the map of South America tacked to my kitchen door,
the swarm of strange names, blue rivers
like veins in an old woman's leg.

A continent I know little about, except what I have read
or my Bolivian neighbor's tales. "A School of Thieves,"
she tells me. "I'd stay home if I were you."

Trapped in front of the hot lights,
I try to forget distances,
how far I will be from the ones who loved me longest.

I do not think anything familiar or cozy.
I think coastlines, jagged edges, roads ahead of me
cracking open like coconuts, and then I smile

Because this face you are snapping
is a map to another continent
I have barely begun to learn.

Touring Mexico with Two Bird Watchers

We wander after the bird watchers like two drugged parrots.
Stare through binoculars—nothing but cloud and blur.
Somehow we have missed the pale-winged Nun Birds
whispering in the tops of trees.

We tune more to civilization, proud men in black suits,
two sombreros asleep on a bench.
I have pledged myself to markets and shacks
while you were out seeking flower vendors,
children tending dolls.
Eyes click into orbit, planets moved by color and light.

South of Matehuala, someone saw a Varied Solitaire
resting on a cactus fence. We saw the fence.

I hunger for detail, yet speak of animals
as if they were all one animal,
one large breathing below the surface of man,
one burrowing, one howl.
I gather shells without knowing what they are called in books.
If the bird watchers ask me what a bird looked like,
I answer, respectfully, "It had—wings."
And feel my ignorance rests somewhere close
to the heart of miracles.

This is the history of Mexico:
A tree splits under the beak of the Splendid Woodpecker.
A Mexican Flicker peacefully spins red wool with straw.
A Squirrel-Cuckoo trembles under the double weight of his name.
High in the mountains, villages composed of Least Antwrens
live happily. They do not know how powerful the other birds can be,
how the Solitary Eagle spreads his giant wings
to circle the lonesome earth.

Listen—tonight the bird watchers are tilting their ears
toward the jungle, the forest, the stars.
A Broad-billed Mourner is about to tell us
the latest episode of evening news
while we, gringos with brightly colored tents and no tail feathers,
peck and nest on the edge of the sky.

Making a Fist

For the first time, on the road north of Tampico,
I felt the life sliding out of me,
a drum in the desert, harder and harder to hear.
I was seven, I lay in the car
watching palm trees swirl a sickening pattern past the glass.
My stomach was a melon split wide inside my skin.

"How do you know if you are going to die?"
I begged my mother.
We had been traveling for days.
With strange confidence she answered,
"When you can no longer make a fist."

Years later I smile to think of that journey,
the borders we must cross separately,
stamped with our unanswerable woes.
I who did not die, who am still living,
still lying in the backseat behind all my questions,
clenching and opening one small hand.

Getting through the Day

From the corners of the city
men are riding toward us on bicycles,
whistling happily.
It is evening.
The streets are ripe bananas.

Our hands had vocations
before they learned to peel and scrub.
No one had to teach them how to love,
where to touch.

This is the hiss the iron makes,
steaming the collars of shirts.
The men are bringing kisses,
a folded note describing our eyes.

It is the message the birds
click in the trees,
someone is coming,
there are people yet to meet
whose names are not written
in the world of the dead.

Guatemala City

One Island

When you meet a man who is satisfied with one island,
you want to walk around him, a complete circumference,
to find where his edges are. If there is sand
or reef—you want to see how the trees grow,
trapped in wind. He shows you the spine
of a sea urchin nested in his foot.
This man whose soul is a boat tied to a single post—
you want to sit with him long enough
to hear the curled shell of your body whistling.
When you say "California" you are a space creature
talking about a star. Nothing grows there.
Here we have mangoes, purple sea-grapes,
hog-plums spilling ripe across a path.
He could show you where to dive to see caves underwater.
The sky is filled with people like you—halfway coming,
halfway going. A plane lands every day between five and six.
The islanders hear it, ears pressed to air,
the minute it leaves the shore. On cloudless days
mountains of the mainland unfurl in the west.
Grocers write proud lists on blackboards beside their doors:
American Cheese, Canned Pork.
Inside are men counting pennies, suspenders ordered in 1968.
There's a lot to do here: walk, watch, breathe.
Yesterday the man found a hunk of driftwood
snagged in the swamp. Hired four friends to drag it out.
Today it becomes a woman listening.
The man drops his chisel, turns her so we can see all sides.
We dream of taking her home with us,
placing her away from the wall in a house far from water.
Why? Because she is like one island,
complete in herself, curves connected.
She only lets you go so far.

After that you are taking the chances
the pirates took, the chances you take every day,
when you live in a world that barely knows you
on a ship that is always pointed
somewhere else.

Utila, Honduras

The Stolen Camera

Since the camera was stolen,
everything is a photograph—
pink bloom against white stucco,
serious face of the potato chip man
leaning over his cart.

In the square, gypsies with brilliant skirts
twirl among palm trees.
I reach for the camera, to hand it to you,
but it is gone, stolen by a thief
who knows nothing of lenses.

Are you thinking of the camera?
I ask you once,
and you nod.
You will not mention it.

Two days ago you caught
the shriveled saint who kissed your hand,
the Twins of Bougainvillea laughing
in their windowsill.
Your camera had careful eyes,
and now the pictures are stolen inside it,
babies who will never be born.

How would I feel if they stole my pens?
My lips would go on making words,
when I crossed the dappled street,
words everywhere, steps
or yellow leaves.

Today we pass the monastery silently.
Maybe we are soaking up light,
brief angles of sun on stone.

Maybe tonight when we sleep
all we have seen will arrange itself
inside us, quick trails of stars,
and we will wake glowing,
the world in our eyes.

Popayan, Colombia

The Only Word a Tree Knows

Tonight the hens line up on a bamboo roost,
sides touching.
You can hold their evening in the palm of a hand,
wondering at restlessness,
the stranger people should never let in.

Pecans falling before we have cracked the ones from last year!
Squirrels building a nest under the roof!
There is nothing to do that isn't singular.
One meal, one letter, one memory roaring inside the head.

The trees promise to remember us.
Yes. It is the only word a tree knows.
Leaves dropping, it is the one thing left.

Tonight we will be branches loose in the wind of our bed,
a motion preceding and following everything we do.

Trees shrink on the wall of the sky.
Listen long enough, they're talking
inside your own head.
This bending, this rake—
a leaf lands, little boat, on the stair.
To be everywhere and know:
I was born to answer a tree.

The Flying Cat

Never, in all your career of worrying, did you imagine
what worries could occur concerning the flying cat.
You are traveling to a distant city.
The cat must travel in a small box with holes.

> Will the baggage compartment be pressurized?
> Will a soldier's footlocker fall on the cat during take-off?
> Will the cat freeze?

You ask these questions one by one, in different voices
over the phone. Sometimes you get an answer,
sometimes a click.
Now it's affecting everything you do.
At dinner you feel nauseous, like you're swallowing
at twenty thousand feet.
In dreams you wave fish-heads, but the cat has grown propellors,
the cat is spinning out of sight!

> Will he faint when the plane lands?
> Is the baggage compartment soundproofed?
> Will the cat go deaf?

"Ma'am, if the cabin weren't pressurized, your cat would explode."
And spoken in a droll impersonal tone, as if
the explosion of cats were another statistic!

Hugging the cat before departure, you realize again
the private language of pain. He purrs. He trusts you.
He knows little of planets or satellites,
black holes in space or the weightless rise of fear.

Burning the Old Year

Letters swallow themselves in seconds.
Notes friends tied to the doorknob,
transparent scarlet paper,
sizzle like moth wings,
marry the air.

So much of any year is flammable,
lists of vegetables, partial poems.
Orange swirling flame of days,
so little is a stone.

Where there was something and suddenly isn't,
an absence shouts, celebrates, leaves a space.
I begin again with the smallest numbers.

Quick dance, shuffle of losses and leaves,
only the things I didn't do
crackle after the blazing dies.

Advice

My great-great-aunt says to plant a tree.
Any nut, she says. She says and says again.
She planted her tree in 1936.

Ahead of us the years loom, forests without histories.
Our hands want to plant something that will bloom tomorrow.
This is too vague, this deep root of ten thousand days.

Don't forget, she says, but we are driving away.
Behind us she brushes a leaf from her step,
sinks a little deeper into the soil of sleep
that has been settling beneath her like a pillow since birth.

Sleeping and Waking

1.
All night someone is trying to tell you something.
The voice is a harbor, pulling you from underneath.

Where am I, you say, what's this and who are you?

The voice washes you up on the shore of your life.
You never knew there was land here.

2.
In the morning you are wakened by gulls.
Flapping at the window, they want you to feed them.
Your eyes blink, your own hands are pulling you back.

All day you break bread into small pieces,
become the tide covering your straight clear tracks.

First Things Last

The kitchen cupboard was my shrine.
I sat cross-legged, removing skillets.

Mama would enter the room, hand to her ear.
Something she had forgotten, the name of a town,
a friend she wanted to call.
Landscapes swirled out from her fingertips,
but this was the Midwest, hopelessly flat and dry.

In my father's voice, a ship was pulling out from port.
Mama fed him lamb chops.
Her eyes were a package lost in the mail.

I wanted to tell them about the double boiler,
but this was before speech.
The way its sacred layers stacked together and fit,
in the cupboard in the corner,
by the mop and the broom.

Famous

The river is famous to the fish.

The loud voice is famous to silence,
which knew it would inherit the earth
before anybody said so.

The cat sleeping on the fence is famous to the birds
watching him from the birdhouse.

The tear is famous, briefly, to the cheek.

The idea you carry close to your bosom
is famous to your bosom.

The boot is famous to the earth,
more famous than the dress shoe,
which is famous only to floors.

The bent photograph is famous to the one who carries it
and not at all famous to the one who is pictured.

I want to be famous to shuffling men
who smile while crossing streets,
sticky children in grocery lines,
famous as the one who smiled back.

I want to be famous in the way a pulley is famous,
or a buttonhole, not because it did anything spectacular,
but because it never forgot what it could do.

The Mother Writes to the Murderer: A Letter

"Alicia didn't like sadness."
The Dallas Morning News

To you whose brain is a blunt fist
pushed deep inside your skull
whose eyes are empty bullets
whose mouth is a stone more speechless
than lost stones at the bottoms of rivers
who lives in a shrunken world where nothing blooms
and no promise is ever kept

To you whose face I never saw but now see
everywhere the rest of my life

You don't know where she hid her buttons

arranged in families by color or size
tissue-wrapped in an oatmeal box
how she told them goodnight   sleep well
and never felt ashamed

You don't know her favorite word
and I won't tell you

You don't have her drawings taped to your refrigerator
blue circuses, red farms
You don't know she cried once in a field of cows
saying they were too beautiful to eat

I'm sure you never thought of that
I'm sure nothing is too beautiful for you to eat

You have no idea what our last words were to one another
how terribly casual

because I thought she was going a block away
with her brother to the store
They would be back in ten minutes

I was ironing her dress
while two houses away an impossible darkness
rose up around my little girl

What can I wish you in return?
I was thinking knives and pistols
high voltages searing off your nerves
I was wishing you could lose your own life
bit by bit   finger by toe
and know what my house is like

how many doors I still will have to open

Maybe worse would be for you to love something
and have it snatched up   sifted out of your sight
for what reason?
a flurry of angels recalled to heaven
and then see how you sit
and move and remember
how you sleep at night
how you feel about mail   my letter to you
all the letters passing through all the hands
of the people on earth
when the only one that matters
is the one you can neither receive
nor send

The Shopper

I visit the grocery store
like an Indian woman of Cuzco
attends the cathedral.
Repeating words:
butter, bread, apples, butter bread apples.

I nod to the grandmothers
muttering among roots.
Their carts tell stories:
they eat little, they live alone.
Last week two women compared their cancers
matter-of-factly as I compare soups.
How do you reach that point of acceptance?
Yes and no shoved in the same basket
and you with a calm face waiting at the check-out stand.

We must bless ourselves with peaches.
Pray to the eggplant, silent among her sisters,
that the seeds will not be bitter on the tongue.
Confess our fears to the flesh of tomato:
we too go forward only halfway ripened
dreaming of the deeper red.

The Hat

"You gotta believe in something or the world's gonna blow up."
Martin Baros, Shiner, Texas

At the Shiner auction, it's not hard to believe in
homemade noodles, ringtailed doves,
Riding on a Railroad quilts.

I can believe the ladies strolling by in knit pants
and cowboy boots have happy marriages
and no one in this town locks doors.

Martin bids on everything and flushes red under the sun.
A blue straw hat sits on his head like a flower.

All day people greet him,
Nice hat, Martin, nice hat.

It's my auction hat, he says proudly.
I only wear it to the auction,
then I save it for the next year.

That night, pedaling home,
I keep thinking about the box in his closet,
the hat going into the box,
the box waiting on the shelf
three hundred sixty-four more days.

Dog

The sky is the belly of a large dog,
sleeping.
All day the small gray flag of his ear
is lowered and raised.
The dream he dreams has no beginning.

Here on earth we dream
a deep-eyed dog sleeps under our stairs
and will rise to meet us.
Dogs curl in dark places,
nests of rich leaves.
We want to bury ourselves
in someone else's home.

The dog who floats over us
has no master.
If there were people who loved him,
he remembers them equally,
the one who smelled like smoke,
the one who brought bones from the restaurant.
It is the long fence
of their hoping he would stay
that he has jumped.

At Portales, New Mexico

They spoke of tumbleweeds
coming to their doors in the night,
whole herds of them scooting across the desert,
arriving at any place there was a wall,
and staying.
In the morning they would rise
to find them stacked,
grazing on air.

Their neighbor tried fire
but his living room went up in flames.
You couldn't fit a tumbleweed in a garbage sack
unless it was a baby one.
If you swept them across the street
they would return to you, loyal,
on the next powerful gust.

What did people do to protect their houses
in New Mexico?
At night they dreamed eastern hedges guarded their beds,
steady lamplight palming each roof.
They never knew they would be planted
on this thin blue line,
nothing between themselves and the next town
but a sign for Indian Gifts.

Where they grew up a root meant something.
Trees lived a hundred years
and bulbs slept secure in the ground.
But here in the West,
the days were flat tables spread with wind,
you never knew who was coming,
how many places to set for dinner;
they had imagined a knock

and opened the door for four big ones,
rolling, right up to the chairs.
You never knew how far your voices would travel
once you let a word out,
felt that curled stem shrinking in your throat
and the thousand directions it could
or could not go.

So Much Happiness

for Michael

It is difficult to know what to do with so much happiness.
With sadness there is something to rub against,
a wound to tend with lotion and cloth.
When the world falls in around you, you have pieces to pick up,
something to hold in your hands, like ticket stubs or change.

But happiness floats.
It doesn't need you to hold it down.
It doesn't need anything.
Happiness lands on the roof of the next house, singing,
and disappears when it wants to.
You are happy either way.
Even the fact that you once lived in a peaceful tree house
and now live over a quarry of noise and dust
cannot make you unhappy.
Everything has a life of its own,
it too could wake up filled with possibilities
of coffee cake and ripe peaches,
and love even the floor which needs to be swept,
the soiled linens and scratched records . . .

Since there is no place large enough
to contain so much happiness,
you shrug, you raise your hands, and it flows out of you
into everything you touch. You are not responsible.
You take no credit, as the night sky takes no credit
for the moon, but continues to hold it, and share it,
and in that way, be known.

Hugging the Jukebox

On an island the soft hue of memory,
moss green, kerosene yellow, drifting, mingling
in the Caribbean Sea,
a six-year-old named Alfred
learns all the words to all the songs
on his grandparents' jukebox, and sings them.
To learn the words is not so hard.
Many barmaids and teenagers have done as well.
But to sing as Alfred sings—
how can a giant whale live in the small pool of his chest?
How can there be breakers this high, notes crashing
at the beach of the throat,
and a reef of coral so enormous only the fishes know its size?

The grandparents watch. They can't sing.
They don't know who this voice is, trapped in their grandson's body.
The boy whose parents sent him back to the island
to chatter mango-talk and scrap with chickens—
three years ago he didn't know the word "sad"!
Now he strings a hundred passionate sentences on a single line.
He bangs his fist so they will raise the volume.

What will they do together in their old age?
It is hard enough keeping yourself alive.
And this wild boy, loving nothing but music—
he'll sing all night, hugging the jukebox.
When a record pauses, that live second before dropping down,
Alfred hugs tighter, arms stretched wide,
head pressed on the luminous belly. "Now!" he yells.
A half-smile when the needle breathes again.

They've tried putting him to bed, but he sings in bed.
Even in Spanish—and he doesn't speak Spanish!

Sings and screams, wants to go back to the jukebox.
O mama I was born with a trumpet in my throat
spent all these years tryin' to cough it up . . .

He can't even read yet. He can't *tell time.*
But he sings, and the chairs in this old dance hall jerk to attention.
The grandparents lean on the counter, shaking their heads.
The customers stop talking and stare, goosey bumps surfacing on their arms.
His voice carries out to the water where boats are tied
and sings for all of them, *a wave.*
For the hens, now roosting in trees,
for the mute boy next door, his second-best friend.
And for the hurricane, now brewing near Barbados—
a week forward neighbors will be hammering boards over their windows,
rounding up dogs and fishing lines,
the generators will quit with solemn clicks in every yard.

But Alfred, hugging a sleeping jukebox, the names of the tunes gone dark,
will still be singing, doubly loud now, teasing his grandmother,
"Put a coin in my mouth!" and believing what she wants to believe;
this is not the end of the island, or the tablets this life has been
scribbled on, or the song.

Utila, Honduras

Yellow Glove

Trying to Name What Doesn't Change

Roselva says the only thing that doesn't change
is train tracks. She's sure of it.
The train changes, or the weeds that grow up spidery
by the side, but not the tracks.
I've watched one for three years, she says,
and it doesn't curve, doesn't break, doesn't grow.

Peter isn't sure. He saw an abandoned track
near Sabinas, Mexico, and says a track without a train
is a changed track. The metal wasn't shiny anymore.
The wood was split and some of the ties were gone.

Every Tuesday on Morales Street
butchers crack the necks of a hundred hens.
The widow in the tilted house
spices her soup with cinnamon.
Ask her what doesn't change.

Stars explode.
The rose curls up as if there is fire in the petals.
The cat who knew me is buried under the bush.

The train whistle still wails its ancient sound
but when it goes away, shrinking back
from the walls of the brain,
it takes something different with it every time.

Hello

Some nights
the rat with pointed teeth
makes his long way back
to the bowl of peaches.
He stands on the dining room table
sinking his tooth
drinking the pulp
of each fruity turned-up face
knowing you will read
this message and scream.
It is his only text,
to take and take in darkness,
to be gone before you awaken
and your giant feet
start creaking the floor.

Where is the mother of the rat?
The father, the shredded nest,
which breath were we taking
when the rat was born,
when he lifted his shivering snout
to rafter and rivet and stone?
I gave him the names of the devil,
seared and screeching names,
I would not enter those rooms
without a stick to guide me,
I leaned on the light, shuddering,
and the moist earth under the house,
the trailing tails of clouds,
said he was in the closet,
the drawer of candles,
his nose was a wick.

How would we live together
with our sad shoes and hideouts,
our lock on the door
and his delicate fingered paws
that could clutch and grip,
his blank slate of fur
and the pillow where we press our faces?
The bed that was a boat is sinking.
And the shores of morning loom up
lined with little shadows,
things we never wanted to be, or meet,
and all the rats are waving hello.

Office 337, Wheeler Hall, Berkeley

I live in a room of abandoned things,
typewriters with jammed ribbons,
clocks that won't wind.
Shelves of books inscribed,
"To Clark, with respect and good wishes."
Clark has moved to another building
without them.

Each day students weave stories
beneath my window.
A boy asks a girl if her interest in him
is growing, and she says, "No."
He should come up and sit
in my office awhile.
Here he could learn what it is to be
a green vinyl chair losing its stuffing.

I like this room so much
I fling the window high
to let the sky in.
Join me, I say.
Whatever leaves us
leaves us both.
I open the door of my heart
so the losses march out.
Now when the call comes
saying my tricky cat is dead,
when the fuschia blossoms
make pink tombs in the grass,
a question I asked years ago
is being answered.

Today a gray nest
fell out of a spruce at my feet.
I lifted it, traced the hollow

where a bird once sat,
and looked up.
The tree was very tall.

I brought the nest to my office,
circled it with eucalyptus leaves
that had also fallen,
fragrant grace notes—
buried my face
in this shrine of knitted twigs
and sang the song
to all things that are gone:
Tu-ra-lu-ra-lu-ra,
it says, you make a short time
seem long.

New Year

Maybe the street is tired of being a street.
They tell how it used to be called Bois d'Arc,
now called Main, how boys in short pants
caught crawdads for supper at a stone acequia
now covered over.
Sometimes the street sweeper stops his machine
and covers his eyes.

Think of the jobs people have.
The girl weighing citron in the basement
of H. L. Green's, for a man who says
he can't wait to make fruitcake
and she says, What is this stuff anyway
before it looks like this? and he leaves
on his cane, slowly, clutching the bag.
Then she weighs garlics for a trucker.

Think of the streams of headlights
on the Houston freeway all headed somewhere
and where they will be headed after that.
After so long, even jets might be tired of acceleration,
slow-down, touching-ground-again,
as a child is so tired of his notebook
he pastes dinosaurs on it to render it extinct.
Or the teacher, tired of questions,
hearing the anthem *How long does it have to be?*
play itself over and over in her sleep
and she just doesn't know. As long as you want it.

What was this world? Where things you never did
felt more real than what happened.
Your friend's dishtowel strung over her faucet
was a sentence which could be diagrammed
while your tumbled life, that basket of phrases,
had too many ways it might fit together.

Where a street might just as easily have been
a hair ribbon in a girl's ponytail
her first day of dance class, teacher in mauve leotard
rising to say, We have much ahead of us,
and the little girls following, kick, kick, kick,
thinking what a proud sleek person she was,
how they wanted to be like her someday,
while she stared outside the window at the high wires
strung with ice, the voices inside them opening out
to every future which was not hers.

Streets

A man leaves the world
and the streets he lived on
grow a little shorter.

One more window dark
in this city, the figs on his branches
will soften for birds.

If we stand quietly enough evenings
there grows a whole company of us
standing quietly together.
Overhead loud grackles are claiming their trees
and the sky which sews and sews, tirelessly sewing,
drops her purple hem.
Each thing in its time, in its place,
it would be nice to think the same about people.

Some people do. They sleep completely,
waking refreshed. Others live in two worlds,
the lost and remembered.
They sleep twice, once for the one who is gone,
once for themselves. They dream thickly,
dream double, they wake from a dream
into another one, they walk the short streets
calling out names, and then they answer.

The House in the Heart

How it is possible to wake this empty
and brew chamomile, watching the water
paint itself yellow and the little flowers
float and bob—

The cars swishing past in dark rain
are going somewhere.
This is my favorite story.
The man with a secret jungle growing
in his brain says chocolate
can make him happy.
I would find a bar
heavy as a brick. With almonds.
And lean forward whispering of
the house in the heart,
the one with penny-size rooms,
moth-wing ceilings, cat-lip doors.

This body we thought so important,
it's a porch, that's all.
I know this, but I don't know
what to do about it.

How it is possible to move
through your own kitchen
touching a bamboo strainer curiously:
Whose is this? And know it is
the one you use every tea,
to feel like an envelope
traveling in and out of the world
carrying messages
and yet not remember
a single one of them—

Today I look out the glass
for some confirmation.
Lights will stay on late this morning.
Palm fronds were frozen last week,
there is rain in the street.
And the house in the heart cries
no one home, no one home.

Old Iron

Some days the words pass us,
cars loaded with vacationers.
We are not going where they are going.
Soon as they top the hill
we'll be on the lost road again,
shouting once, then listening,
kicking a stone toward
anything like a tree.

Then the first language crawls back
into the ears, humming.
A twig scratches two words
in damp red earth:
NO   THOUGHT.
I'm looking for cedar stumps,
a black calf in a blue field,
anything to report
that has nothing to do with my life.

I'm looking for the rusted skillet
hunters left hanging on a branch.
Years after they sighed in firelight
the tree claims their old iron
as another natural arm.

The White Road

I can't even count
how many of my own feet
walk the white stone road today.
As if the feet of past years
tramped alongside,
and the future feet,
anchors already forming
in the sea of blood,
accompanied.
Why should such a simple sadness
well up like a crowd?

Now I've even forgotten
whose sadness it was to begin with.
Maybe it belongs to the nun
who waits for the 6 A.M. bus,
whose headscarf is white
and always tied.
Maybe she feels lighter today
having dropped it.
Or the man at the state hospital
who kept singing
"These are a few of my favorite things"
though his cigarette trembled
and he wore pajamas in the afternoon—

These stones have smooth backs.
They could be praying, or sleeping.
I could be anyone else,
researching sadness,
finding out how it adheres to the world,
bubbling and thickening, flour in broth,
how women who have lost children
sometimes feel like women
who have lost homes in fires

or men in their fifties who feel
the days shrinking in front of them
sometimes weep for a neighbor boy's dog.

Dew

A Kickapoo grandmother pulled
deerhide moccasins out of her bosom,
said, If you really want these
to fit your feet,
walk in the dew a little,
walk in the dew.

She lived in a cattail hut
ringed by mountains.
There was no road to her house.

I think of her every day
as I touch the forks and curtains,
the pens and melons
that line this life,
feeling how we grow together,
things and the life beyond things,
one gradually fitted motion
moving home across the grass.

The Use of Fiction

A boy claims he saw you on a bicycle last week,
touring his neighborhood. "West Cypress Street!" he shouts,
as if your being there and his seeing you
were some sort of benediction.
To be alive, to be standing outside
on a tender February evening . . .
"It was a blue bicycle, ma'am, your braid was flying,
I said hello and you laughed, remember?"

You almost tell him your bicycle seat is thick with dust,
the tires have been flat for months.
But his face, that radiant flower, says you are his friend,
he has told his mother your name.
Maybe this is a clear marble
he will hide in his sock drawer for months.
So who now, in a universe of figures,
would deny West Cypress Street,
throwing up clouds into this literal sky?
"Yes, amigo"—hand on shoulder—
"It was I."

Moon Trio

1.
Moon of silence, unexpected visitor.
Quickly I leave what I was doing.
Half-sentences roll back into themselves like drawers.
I will give you the smoothest pillow,
the blue glass from Mexico which certain light
can change to sky.

2.
A man from the Zuni reservation
makes parties for the full moon.
He toasts the glowing mesa,
friends arrive and orbit the floor.

Here's one party where the honored guest
brings the gift.

3.
Alfredo in red socks
under a sliver of moon
is doing his job, occupying steps.
For years he has said, "Could be better,
could be worse."
Tonight he is quiet, cigarette
balanced on lips.
His friend Maria, More-Than-99, babbles
excitedly in Spanish, white nightgown
billowing out around her as if she were swimming
and the air held it up.

Moon topping chimney.

Maria, More-Than-99, says,
"We will paint this house."

Defining White

On the telephone no one knows what white is.
My husband knows, he takes pictures.
He has whole notebooks defining
how white is white, is black,
and all the gray neighborhoods in between.

The telephone is blind.
Cream-white? Off-white?
I want a white, he says,
that is white-white,
that tends in no direction
other than itself.

Now this is getting complex.
Every white I see is tending
toward something else.
The house was white, but it is peeling.
People are none of these colors.

In the sky white sentences form and detach.
Who speaks here? What breath
scrawls itself endlessly,
white on white, without being heard?
Is wind a noun or a verb?

Sure

Today you rain on me from every corner of the sky.
Softly vanishing hair, a tiny tea set from Mexico
perched on a shelf with the life-size cups.

I remember knotting my braid on your bed,
ten months into your silence.
Someone said you were unreachable,
we could chatter and you wouldn't know.
You raised yourself on magnificent dying elbows
to speak one line,
"Don't—be—so—sure."
The room was stunned.
Lying back on your pillow, you smiled at me.
No one else saw it.
Later they even denied they heard.

All your life, never mind.
It hurts, but never mind.
You fed me corn from cans, stirring busily.
I lined up the salt shakers on your table.
We were proud of each other for nothing.
You, because I finished my meal.
Me, because you wore a flowered dress.
Life was a tablet of small reasons.
"That's that," you'd say, pushing back your chair.
"And now let's go see if the bakery has a cake."

Today, as I knelt to spell a word for a boy,
it was your old floor under me,
cool sections of black and white tile,
I'd lie on my belly tracing their sides.
St. Louis, movies sold popcorn,
baby lions born in zoos,
the newspapers would never find us.

One moth lighting on the sink
in a dark apartment years ago.
You point, should I catch it?
Oh, never mind.
A million motions later, I open my hand,
and it is there.

Going for Peaches, Fredericksburg, Texas

Those with experience look for a special kind.
Red Globe, the skin slips off like a fine silk camisole.
Boy breaks one open with his hands. Yes, it's good,
my old relatives say, but we'll look around.
They want me to stop at every peach stand
between Stonewall and Fredericksburg,
leave the air conditioner running,
jump out and ask the price.

Coming up here they talked about
the best ways to die. One favors a plane crash,
but not over a city. One wants to make sure
her grass is watered when she goes.
Ladies, ladies! This peach is fine,
it blushes on both sides.
But they want to keep driving.

In Fredericksburg the houses are stone,
they remind me of wristwatches, glass polished,
years ticking by in each wall.
I don't like stone, says one. What if it fell?
I don't like Fredericksburg, says the other.
Too many Germans driving too slow.
She herself is German as Stuttgart.
The day presses forward wearing complaints,
charms on its bony wrist.

Actually ladies, (I can't resist),
I don't think you wanted peaches after all,
you just wanted a nip of scenery,
some hills to tuck behind your heads.
The buying starts immediately, from a scarfed woman
who says she gave up teachin' for peachin'.
She has us sign a guest book.
One aunt insists on reloading into her box

to see the fruit on the bottom.
One rejects any slight bruise.
But Ma'am, the seller insists, nature isn't perfect.
Her hands are spotted, like a peach.

On the road, cars weave loose patterns between lanes.
We will float in flowery peach-smell
back to our separate kettles, our private tables
and knives, and line up the bounty,
deciding which ones go where.
A canned peach, says one aunt, lasts ten years.
She was 87 last week. But a frozen peach
tastes better on ice cream.
Everything we have learned so far,
skins alive and ripening, on a day
that was real to us, that was summer,
motion going out and memory coming in.

The Thinly Fluted Wings of Stamps

Birds spoke your language by coming to the sill.
Letters cooperated by flying away.
You tore white strips from the hearts of loaves.

The birds were nouns, you could say,
"I saw three gnat-catchers, seventeen cardinals,"
and make a place in the air that was yours.
They brought you whatever their feet had touched,
branch, birdbath, red interlocking roof,
and all the words that mean flight:
dodge, glide, soar.
Fifteen years you nested in one room,
one fluffy pink sweater, without coming downstairs.

I laughed at your letters. "Prince Charles
is still available. Satan sleeps in the White House,
please write back soon." I still laugh.
You were the only person I knew who used real ink.

At night you wondered where the birds were sleeping,
felt their small breath hovering in your bones and hair.
You dreamed your clock became an onion,
sprouting one green shoot.
You were hungry, but wouldn't cut it.
Once I visited you and curtains were flapping,
the sky had eyes. "They need me. The birds need me."
A truck from the bakery delivered twenty loaves.
Every day? You nodded. You said we all had our jobs.

Now I feel your small flights nudging me.
A hundred blackbirds fly north, toward Chicago.
I think maybe they knew you and stand still for a moment,
staring up. This is our ongoing correspondence,

the wing between our worlds: to stoop for small things,
scatter seed for hens, notice the feather has two sides.
There are crazier ways. *Prince Charles taken.*
I lined six stones in the sill and have been watching them
for days.

Yellow Glove

What can a yellow glove mean in a world of motorcars and
governments?

I was small, like everyone. Life was a string of precautions: Don't
kiss the squirrel before you bury him, don't suck candy, pop balloons,
drop watermelons, watch TV. When the new gloves appeared one
Christmas, tucked in soft tissue, I heard it trailing me: Don't lose
the yellow gloves.

I was small, there was too much to remember. One day, waving at a
stream—the ice had cracked, winter chipping down, soon we would
sail boats and roll into ditches—I let a glove go. Into the stream,
sucked under the street. Since when did streets have mouths?
I walked home on a desperate road. Gloves cost money. We didn't
have much. I would tell no one. I would wear the yellow glove that
was left and keep the other hand in a pocket. I knew my mother's
eyes had tears they had not cried yet, I didn't want to be the one
to make them flow. It was the prayer I spoke secretly, folding socks,
lining up donkeys in windowsills. *To be good*, a promise made to
the roaches who scouted my closet at night. *If you don't get in my
bed, I will be good.* And they listened. I had a lot to fulfill.

The months rolled down like towels out of a machine. I sang and
drew and fattened the cat. Don't scream, don't lie, don't cheat, don't
fight—you could hear it anywhere. A pebble could show you how to
be smooth, tell the truth. A field could show how to sleep without
walls. A stream could remember how to drift and change—next
June I was stirring the stream like a soup, telling my brother dinner
would be ready if he'd only hurry up with the bread, when I saw it.
The yellow glove draped on a twig. A muddy survivor. A quiet flag.

Where had it been in the three gone months? I could wash it, fold it in my winter drawer with its sister, no one in that world would ever know. There were miracles on Harvey Street. Children walked home in yellow light. Trees were reborn and gloves traveled far, but returned. A thousand miles later, what can a yellow glove mean in a world of bankbooks and stereos?

Part of the difference between floating and going down.

The Brick

Each morning in the gray margin
between sleep and rising, I find myself
on Pershing Avenue, St. Louis, examining bricks
in buildings, looking for the one I brushed
with my mitten in 1956. How will I know it
when I find it? A shade goes up in one window.
This is where the man in the undershirt lived.
Someone shakes a coffee can and turns a faucet;
water gushes out, ice-cold.
Why do I want this brick? What does a brick,
red or otherwise, have to tell anyone
about how to live a life? It's as crazy
as crying for a bear when you were three,
those little hands hopefully touching the nose,
maybe they even named it. "Fuzzy."
So what could I name a brick? Hard.
What Buildings Are Made Of.
And why would one brick that I brushed
while on a walk with my mother and father
become a shrine? Later we rode a bus.
My father carried a sack from a drugstore.
I stared hard at the faces of shops
to see what they looked like in the dark.
And things went on that way for decades,
doors opening, buzzers going off,
someone saying, "We're almost there."

So. This has something to do with why
I stare at certain buildings in any city.
I don't know where the mittens went,
they had a cord to keep them together.
I'm sure my parents could drive down

Pershing Avenue tomorrow without weeping.
But it's different for me.
It's the snagged edge, the center of memory,
the place where I get off and on.

Breaking My Favorite Bowl

Some afternoons
thud unexpectedly
and split into four pieces
on the floor.

Two large pieces, two small ones.
I could glue them back,
but what would I use them for?

Forgive me when I answer you
in a voice so swollen
it won't fit your ears.

I'm thinking about apples and histories,
the hands I broke off
my mother's praying statue
when I was four—
how she tearfully repaired them,
but the hairline cracks
in the wrists
were all she said
she could see—

the unannounced blur
of something passing
out of a life.

Blood

"A true Arab knows how to catch a fly in his hands,"
my father would say. And he'd prove it,
cupping the buzzer instantly
while the host with the swatter stared.

In the spring our palms peeled like snakes.
True Arabs believed watermelon could heal fifty ways.
I changed these to fit the occasion.

Years before, a girl knocked,
wanted to see the Arab.
I said we didn't have one.
After that, my father told me who he was,
"Shihab"—"shooting star"—
a good name, borrowed from the sky.
Once I said, "When we die, we give it back?"
He said that's what a true Arab would say.

Today the headlines clot in my blood.
A little Palestinian dangles a truck on the front page.
Homeless fig, this tragedy with a terrible root
is too big for us. What flag can we wave?
I wave the flag of stone and seed,
table mat stitched in blue.

I call my father, we talk around the news.
It is too much for him,
neither of his two languages can reach it.
I drive into the country to find sheep, cows,
to plead with the air:
Who calls anyone *civilized*?
Where can the crying heart graze?
What does a true Arab do now?

Lunch in Nablus City Park

When you lunch in a town which has recently known war
under a calm slate sky mirroring none of it,
certain words feel impossible in the mouth.
Casualty: too casual, it must be changed.
A short man stacks mounds of pita bread
on each end of the table, muttering
something about more to come.
Plump birds landing on park benches
surely had their eyes closed recently,
must have seen nothing of weapons or blockades.
When the woman across from you whispers
I don't think we can take it anymore
and you say there are people praying for her
in the mountains of Himalaya and she says
Lady, it is not enough, then what?

A plate of cigar-shaped meatballs, dish of tomato,
friends dipping bread—
I will not marry till there is true love, says one,
throwing back her cascade of perfumed hair.
He says the University of Texas seems remote to him
as Mars, and last month he stayed in his house
for 26 days. He will not leave, he refuses to leave.
In the market they are selling
men's shoes with air vents, a beggar displays
the giant scab of leg he must drag from alley to alley,
and students gather to discuss what constitutes
genuine protest.

In summers, this cafe is full.
Today only our table sends laughter into the trees.
What cannot be answered checkers the tablecloth
between the squares of white and red.
Where do the souls of hills hide
when there is shooting in the valleys?

What makes a man with a gun seem bigger
than a man with almonds? How can there be war
and the next day eating, a man stacking plates
on the curl of his arm, a table of people
toasting one another in languages of grace:
For you who came so far;
For you who held out, wearing a black scarf
to signify grief;
For you who believe true love can find you
amidst this atlas of tears linking one town
to its own memory of mortar,
when it was still a dream to be built
and people moved here, believing,
and someone with sky and birds in his heart
said this would be a good place for a park.

The Garden of Abu Mahmoud

He had also lived in Spain
so we stood under a glossy loquat tree
telling of *madres y milagros*
with clumsy tongues.
It seemed strange in the mouth
of this Arab, but no more so
than everything.
Across his valley the military
settlement gleamed white.
He said, That's where the guns live,
as simply as saying, it needs sun,
a plant needs sun.
He stooped to unsheathe an eggplant
from its nest of leaves,
purple shining globe,
and pressed it on me.
I said No, no, I don't want
to take things before they are ripe,
but it was started already,
handfuls of marble-sized peaches,
hard green *mish-mish* and delicate lilt
of beans. Each pocket swelled
as he breathed mint leaves,
bit the jagged edge.
He said every morning found him here,
before the water boiled on the flame
he came out to this garden,
dug hands into earth saying, I know you
and earth crumbled rich layers
and this result of their knowing—
a hillside in which no inch went unsung.
His enormous onions held light
and the trees so weighted with fruits
he tied the branches up.

And he called it *querido, corazon*,
all the words of any language
connecting to the deep place
of darkness and seed. He called it
ya habibi in Arabic, my darling tomato,
and it called him governor, king,
and some days he wore no shoes.

West Bank

Jerusalem

Two girls danced, red flames winding.
I offered my shoes to the gypsies,
threw back my head, and yelled.

All day their hillocks of cheese
had been drying on a goat hide
stretched in the sun.
So it was true—they came in the night,
they set their dark tents flapping.
Gypsies see right through you,
I'd heard a man say in town.
And did they like what they saw?

To live without roads seemed one way
not to get lost. To make maps
of stone and grass, to rub stars together
and find a spark.

I gave American shoes, sandals from Greece.
They held each one curiously, shy to put them on.
Later the shoes disappeared into the tent
and I walked home with their drums in my belly.
Maybe they would use them as vases,
drawers. At least there were choices,
not like a sword, which did only one thing,
or a house, which sat and sat in the desert
after the goats and music had blown away.

The Man Who Makes Brooms

So you come with these maps in your head
and I come with voices chiding me to
"speak for my people"
and we march around like guardians of memory
till we find the man on the short stool
who makes brooms.

Thumb over thumb, straw over straw,
he will not look at us.
In his stony corner there is barely room
for baskets and thread,
much less the weight of our faces
staring at him from the street.
What he has lost or not lost is his secret.

You say he is like all the men,
the man who sells pistachios,
the man who rolls the rugs.
Older now, you find holiness in anything
that continues, dream after dream.
I say he is like nobody,
the pink seam he weaves
across the flat golden face of this broom
is its own shrine, and forget about the tears.

In the village the uncles will raise their *kefiyahs*
from dominoes to say, no brooms in America?
And the girls who stoop to sweep the courtyard
will stop for a moment and cock their heads.
It is a little song, this thumb over thumb,
but sometimes when you wait years
for the air to break open
and sense to fall out,
it may be the only one.

Jerusalem

Mother of Nothing

Sister, the stars have no children.
The stars pecking at each night's darkness
above your trailer would shine back at themselves
in its metal, but they are too far away.
The stones lining your path to the goats
know themselves only as speechless, flat,
gray-in-the-sun.
What begins and ends in the self
without continuance in any other.

You who stand at preschool fences
watching the endless tumble and slide,
who answer the mothers' Which one is yours?
with blotted murmur and turning away,
listen. Any lack carried
too close to the heart
grows teeth, nibbles off
corners. I heard one say
she had no talent,
another, no time, and there were many
without beauty all those years,
and all of them shrinking.
What sinks to the bottom of the pond
comes up with new colors, or not at all.

We sank, and there was purple,
voluptuous merging of purple and blue,
a new silence living
in the houses of our bodies.
Those who wanted and never received,
who were born without hands,
who had and then lost; the Turkish mother
after the earthquake
with five silent children lined before her,

the women of Beirut
bearing water to their bombed-out rooms,
the fathers in offices
with framed photographs of children on their desks,
and their own private knowledge
of all the hard words.

And we held trees differently
then, and dried plates differently,
because waiting dulls the senses
and when you are no longer waiting,
something wakes up. My cousin said
It's not children, it's a matter of making
life. And I saw the streets opening into the future,
cars passing, mothers with car seats,
children waving out the rear window,
keeping count of all who waved back,
and would we lift our hearts and answer them,
and when we did, what would we say?
And the old preposterous stories of nothing
and everything finally equalling one another
returned in the night. And like relatives,
knew where the secret key was hidden
and let themselves in.

Arabic Coffee

It was never too strong for us:
make it blacker, Papa,
thick in the bottom,
tell again how the years will gather
in small white cups,
how luck lives in a spot of grounds.

Leaning over the stove, he let it
boil to the top, and down again.
Two times. No sugar in his pot.
And the place where men and women
break off from one another
was not present in that room.
The hundred disappointments,
fire swallowing olive-wood beads
at the warehouse, and the dreams
tucked like pocket handkerchiefs
into each day, took their places
on the table, near the half-empty
dish of corn. And none was
more important than the others,
and all were guests. When
he carried the tray into the room,
high and balanced in his hands,
it was an offering to all of them,
stay, be seated, follow the talk
wherever it goes. The coffee was
the center of the flower.
Like clothes on a line saying
You will live long enough to wear me,
a motion of faith. There is this,
and there is more.

The Traveling Onion

"It is believed that the onion originally came from India. In Egypt it was an object of worship—why I haven't been able to find out. From Egypt the onion entered Greece and on to Italy, thence into all of Europe."

Better Living Cookbook

When I think how far the onion has traveled
just to enter my stew today, I could kneel and praise
all small forgotten miracles,
crackly paper peeling on the drainboard,
pearly layers in smooth agreement,
the way knife enters onion
and onion falls apart on the chopping block,
a history revealed.

And I would never scold the onion
for causing tears.
It is right that tears fall
for something small and forgotten.
How at meal, we sit to eat,
commenting on texture of meat or herbal aroma
but never on the translucence of onion,
now limp, now divided,
or its traditionally honorable career:
For the sake of others,
disappear.

Telling the Story

In America, what's real
juggles with what isn't:
a woman I know props fabulous tulips
in her flowerbed, in snow.

Streets aren't gold, but they could be.
Once a traveler mailed letters
in a trashcan for a week.
He thought they were going somewhere.
In America everything is going somewhere.

I answered a telephone
on a California street.
Hello? It was possible.
A voice said, "There is no scientific proof
that God is a man."
"Thank you." I was standing there.
Was this meant for me?
It was not exactly the question
I had been asking, but it kept me busy awhile,
telling the story.

Some start out
with a big story
that shrinks.

Some stories accumulate power
like a sky gathering clouds,
quietly, quietly,
till the story rains around you.

Some get tired of the same story
and quit speaking;
a farmer leaning into
his row of potatoes,

a mother walking the same child
to school.
What will we learn today?
There should be an answer,
and it should
change.

Two Countries

Skin remembers how long the years grow
when skin is not touched, a gray tunnel
of singleness, feather lost from the tail
of a bird, swirling onto a step,
swept away by someone who never saw
it was a feather. Skin ate, walked,
slept by itself, knew how to raise a
see-you-later hand. But skin felt
it was never seen, never known as
a land on the map, nose like a city,
hip like a city, gleaming dome of the mosque
and the hundred corridors of cinnamon and rope.

Skin had hope, that's what skin does.
Heals over the scarred place, makes a road.
Love means you breathe in two countries.
And skin remembers—silk, spiny grass,
deep in the pocket that is skin's secret own.
Even now, when skin is not alone,
it remembers being alone and thanks something larger
that there are travelers, that people go places
larger than themselves.

At Mother Teresa's

Finally there are enough people to hug!
A room of two-year-olds with raised arms . . .
we swing them into the air,
their grins are windows
in a city of crumbling walls.
One girl stays in the corner
crouched over her shoes.
Hard to keep shoes in this world,
people steal them, they walk away.
Her flaming hair is a house
she lives in all alone.
When I touch it she looks up,
suspicious, then lifts
a stub of chalk from her shoe.
Makes three jagged lines on the floor.
Can I read? I nod rapidly,
imagining *love me, love me, yes,*
but she is too alone to believe it.
Her face closes. I will never guess.

Calcutta

The Endless Indian Nights

How the same Shah who commanded thousands
to build the Taj Mahal could later be jailed for life
by a single son is something to think about
during the endless Indian nights.
In the stump of candle,
a crooked wick keeps sinking.
I press my lips to your back.
All night the tiresome anklet of charms and voices:
no no no, three times, the way they say in Asia,
or the Goan priest who wrote a farewell letter in couplets.
He even spoke in rhyme and could rhyme with Ghandi.
On the table our tea was deep, and true.

Everywhere camels plunge to their knees
and pretend there are no people.
A villager asked me, "What is your caste?"
"We don't have castes in America." He stared harder.
"Then how do you know who you are?"

Tonight I would laugh less,
I would place my hands together and ask
how he sleeps in this populous dark.
On the boulevard from earth to moon
our wings are dragging.
The babies of Calcutta, bearers with empty baskets,
sorrowful fringe of the robe—how many times
do we put you on? It was dark, then it was dark again.
It was dark so long we thought the day was lost.
I lay thinking of Afghanistan, men who live in caves
eating potatoes till their faces grow longer,
their eyes blacken and will not close.
Someone said the world has never forgotten anyone
better. And I vowed to remember them
though what good it would do, who knows.

At dawn a cook wept in the kitchen,
once he cooked for Maharajah and now he cooked for pigs.
I thanked him so many times for his omelette.
He wanted letters from America saying
he was a good cook. I promised,
the morning unwrapped its shining turban
and flung it wide, so we dreamed we were done
with sleeping. It reached a new momentum,
like a professor who keeps writing onto the wall
after he fills the blackboard and the students,
startled, pay better attention. *What is this?*
Because now that there are no borders
they could imagine him continuing onto their desks,
their innocent skin.

No One Thinks of Tegucigalpa

No one thinks of Tegucigalpa, unless you are the man
at the Christmas party who sells weapons to Honduras
and smilingly bets on war. Or you have been there,
you wear the miles of markets, a cascading undergarment
beneath your calm white shirt, the slick black tiles
of the plaza, a girl coming early, little hum and bucket,
to polish them. Near the river, a toothless man kept
parrots and monkeys in his yard. *¿Por que?* He said, "Love."

They don't want to hear about Tegucigalpa because it makes
them feel like a catalogue of omissions. Where is it?
Now who? As if Houston were everything, the sun comes up
because commerce exists . . . But if you kept driving south,
past Mexico's pointed peaks, the grieving villages of
Guatemala, you would reach the city that climbs hills,
opening its pink-lidded eye while the Peace Monument
draws a quiet breath. A boy stands all day skewering
lean squares of beef till the night hisses on his grill.

Where is it? At the end of the arm, so close I tap the
red roofs with my finger, the basket seller weaves a
crib for my heart. Think of the countries you have never
seen, the cities of those countries, start here, then ask:
How bad is it to dress in a cold room? How small your own
wish for a parcel of children? How remarkably invisible
this tear?

What Is Given, What Is Not Given

"Not sadness, which is always there . . ."
    Phillip Lopate

To market, you hens with stunned faces,
crate of papaya, peanuts and corn.
Cart wheels fit the ruts in the road.
I stand back, a shadow.
Men who know each other are saying Good Day.
All my life I wanted to find the simplest
cleanest way of doing anything.
Something to plant in the heart—
a belief, a grove of trees.
Lost in the city of blue doors,
cloud cap on the mountain,
why should anyone nod?
Inside each memory shadows are the shrine.

On Chiapa de Corzo women line up for tortillas,
their faces soft with peace.
Maybe we read each other wrong.
Time which never fits the face I give it,
which always seems too short or too long,
how do I become your servant now?
My basket is small, it fits one finger.
After the market, mounds of withered leaves.

When will legs equal the streets
strung out before them?
Each year I listen harder
to hear it, corners whispering
Don't worry you will grow.

Pakistan with Open Arms

Tonight in Karachi, a man drapes
jasmine garlands over his wrist
and looks both ways.
It is the hour of the walk,
when men and women come slowly forth
from houses, kitchens,
their stride growing long and musical,
sky finally softening its grip.
Whatever they talked about in the day
stands back to let them pass.

In some languages, a voice asking
a question goes up at the end
and an answer slopes toward the sea.
Maybe now the turtles are stepping
from their nests at the beach,
the huge shrine of their eggs behind them.
Maybe the fabulous painted buses
are cooling their engines at the lot.

How could I have seen, twenty years ago,
a night when a string of fragrant flowers
would be all I desired?
In the peaked shadow of his house
a man reads a map on which deserts
and mountains are different colors.
Each province has its own woven rugs
and speckled red hats.
He wishes to walk in a hundred villages
where people he will never meet are walking.

Into my arms I gather the quiet avenue,
the patience of curbs.
A family relaxes on a sweep of public grass.
Their shirts are cotton and silk.

They visit quietly as the moon comes speaking
its simple round name.
I gather them into me, saying,
This is the thunderous city.
This is the person who once was afraid.

With the Greeks

for Dan and Chrissie Anthony

When you dance Greek-style,
you wave a handkerchief,
the foot stomps, a necklace of islands
rises in the blood.
Moving through days,
the shadow of this circle
stays with you.
Outline of a wheeling fish
that says you are less alone
than you like to think.

At the grill, shrimp curl perfectly
on sticks. A sleek woman with a bow tie
strokes her husband's hand.
What have we in common?
Grandmother spooning honey-puffs
smiles at anyone, Here child, eat,
fortify yourself for the journey
between homes.

Floating heart, who knows
which hand is on which arm?
Whether any story begins or ends
where we say it does
or goes on like a circle,
common sea between stones and lamps.
In the villages of Greece,
windows light up, eyes.
Children carry things in baskets.
A basket sits on a floor.

I heard of an orchard where statues grew up
between the roots of trees. Stones were men,

one trunk had feet. I heard of an island
where snails rose from the dirt
and saved the people, who were starving.

Tonight there is no ocean
that does not sing. Even sorrow,
which we have felt and felt again
in all our lands, has hands.

Where the Soft Air Lives

"Meanwhile Dean and I went out to dig the streets of Mexican San
Antonio. It was fragrant and soft—the softest air I'd ever known—and
dark, and mysterious, and buzzing. Sudden figures of girls in white
bandannas appeared in the humming dark."
  Jack Kerouac, *On the Road*

1.
She placed her babies in the sink
stroking off the heat with an old damp rag.
Coo-coo little birdies, she sang,
then she tied the hair up in ponytails
pointing to the moon. It made them look
like little fruits with a pointed end.
She said, You don't think about poverty
till someone comes over.

2.
The man on Guadalupe Street is
guarding the cars. On his porch
the lights of Virgin Mary flash
endlessly, prayer-time, vigilante,
he rocks with his wife every night
rocking, while the bakery seals its cases
of pumpkin tart and the boys
with T-shirts slashed off below the nipples
strut big as buses past his gate.
He is keeping an eye on them.
And on fenders, hubcaps,
a grocery cart let loose
and lodged against a fence.
Cars roar past, but they will have
to go home again. He is happy
in this life, blinking Mother of God,
his wife placing one curl of mint in the tea,

saying always the same line,
Is it sweet enough? and the porch
painted three shades of green.

3.
I mended my ways, he said.
I took a needle and big thread and mended them.
You would not know me to see me now.
Sometimes I see myself sweeping the yard,
watering the dog, and I think
who is that guy? He looks like an old guy.
He looks like a guy who tells you
fifteen dead stories and mixes them up.
So that explains it:
why I don't tell you nuthin.

4.
She feeds her roses coffee
to make them huge. When her son was in Vietnam
the bougainvillea turned black once overnight.
But he didn't die. She prescribes lemongrass,
manzanilla: in her album the grandchildren
smile like seed packets.
She raises the American flag on her pole
because she is her own Mexican flag
and the wind fluttering the hem of her dress
says there is no border in the sky.

5.
Lisa's husband left, so she dyed her hair
a different color every day. Once pale silk,
next morning, a flame. She shaped her nails,
wore a nightgown cut down so low
the great canyon between her bosoms
woke up the mailman dragging his bag.

She pulled the bed into the dining room,
placed it dead center, never went out.
TV, eyelash glue, pools of perfume.
She was waiting for the plumber,
the man who sprays the bugs. Waiting
to pay a newspaper bill, to open her arms,
unroll all her front pages
and the sad unread sections too,
the ads for bacon and cleanser,
the way they try to get you to come to the store
by doubling your coupons,
the way they line the ads in red.

6.
Air filled with hearts,
we pin them to our tongues,
follow the soft air back to its cave
between trees, river of air
pouring warm speech, two-colored speech
into the streets. *Make a house
and live in it.*

At the Mission Espada
the priest keeps a little goat
tied to a stump.
His people come slowly out
of the stone-white room,
come lifting their feet suddenly heavy,
trying to remember far back before
anything had happened twice.
Someone lit a candle, and it caught.
A girl in a white dress,
singing in a window.
And you were getting married,

getting born, seeing the slice of blue
that meant *shore*;
the goat rises,
his bitten patch of land around him.
The priest bends to touch his head.
And goes off somewhere.
But the air behind him
still holding that hand, and the little goat
still standing.

The Man Who Hated Trees

When he started blaming robberies
on trees, you knew for sure
something was wrong.

This man who clipped hair,
who spent years shaving the necks
of cafeteria managers,
sweeping lost curls down drains,
this man who said, "It is always better
to cut off a little too much . . ."

You could say he transferred
one thing to another when he came home,
hair to leaves, only this time
he was cutting down whole bodies,
from the feet up, he wanted
to make those customers stumps.

One tree dropped purple balls
on the roof of his car.
One tree touched the rain gutter.
He didn't like blossoms, too much mess.
"Trees take up the sky.
It's my light, why share it?"
He said thieves struck more
on blocks where there were trees.
"The shade, you know. They like the dark."
You lived for days with the buzz of his chain saw
searing off the last little branches of neighborly affection.

It was planting season in the rest of the town
but your street received a crew cut.
Two pecan trees that had taken half a century to rise
now stood like Mohawk Indians, shorn.

He gloated on his porch surrounded by amputations.
You caught him staring greedily
at the loose branches swinging over your roof.

Tomorrow, when everything was cut, what then?
He joked about running over cats
as the last chinaberry crashed,
as the truck came to gather arms and legs
waggling their last farewell.

What stories did he tell himself,
this patriot of springtime,
and how did it feel to drive down sprouting boulevards
with his bald, bald heart?

Rain

A teacher asked Paul
what he would remember
from third grade, and he sat
a long time before writing
"this year sumbody tutched me
on the sholder"
and turned his paper in.
Later she showed it to me
as an example of her wasted life.
The words he wrote were large
as houses in a landscape.
He wanted to go inside them
and live, he could fill in
the windows of "o" and "d"
and be safe while outside
birds building nests in drainpipes
knew nothing of the coming rain.

You Have to Be Careful

You have to be careful telling things.
Some ears are tunnels.
Your words will go in and get lost in the dark.
Some ears are flat pans like the miners used
looking for gold.
What you say will be washed out with the stones.

You look a long time till you find the right ears.
Till then, there are birds and lamps to be spoken to,
a patient cloth rubbing shine in circles,
and the slow, gradually growing possibility
that when you find such ears,
they already know.

Over the Fence

It is no miracle, she says.
A husband drives away,
the world clicks shut
like a little dead door.
If I could go to a movie
that lasted longer than my life
it might be alright.

I was born on this street,
the man who shot himself in your bathroom
was my first friend.
My mother closed the shades
when the ambulance came.
A dish is dirty, is clean, is dirty,
what song is this if
it's the only one you know?

Don't tell the trashmen
I'm here alone.
Tell them we're late sleepers,
the curtains stay shut
so we can live like kings.

On your side of the fence
iris float their silken heads.
Over here the rose is a stick forever.

You say I'm lucky to know
two languages. What good are two words
if no one can hear them?
I'd take one tongue if it fit me,
I'd wear it like the postman
wears his suit, so people know
what he is doing in the world.

Walk up and down the street
delivering smiles.
I say no one is lucky.
We have faces, they get old.

French Movies

in memory of Patrick Dewaere

1.
Roasted chicken placed on a linen cloth.
In the movie it is still sitting there.
You forgot to eat it. We go outside to find
glass bottles smashed behind our cars.

2.
In some men the future is written
with a definite pen.
He strides out of here,
heading into the future.

You were a page of mist,
hovering. Your voice said
other people's words,
erased its own.

How they explained it:
He was fragile,
couldn't face reality.

One radiant tear in a train station—
even today, all our ages stand still
in your face. It is impossible
to blink.

3.
I wish I could have held on
to your coattails.
We could have stood with the other half-sure ones
near the lighthouse in the tourist town
listening to wave and cloud,
the way no script written there
survives, and who worries about it?

Then when they stood in line to say
this world was not enough, perhaps
you would not be among them.
Knowing that story already,
you could make a different one.
The French critic reminds us
the French like their movies ambiguous.

4.
Here in a country of real estate and sun,
you visit only briefly.
Materialize on the screen,
then whisk away,
leaving us pale shoulders,
slightly balding spot on the back of the skull,
maps to a country which no longer exists.
I wish your coattails had been longer.
If we are not fragile, we don't deserve the world.

Catalogue Army

Something has happened to my name.
It now appears on catalogues
for towels and hiking equipment,
dresses spun in India,
hand-colored prints of parrots and eggs.
Fifty tulips are on their way
if I will open the door.
Dishrags from North Carolina
unstack themselves in the Smoky Mountains
and make a beeline for my sink.

I write a postcard to my cousin:
this is what it is like to live in America.
Individual tartlet pans congregate
in the kitchen, chiming my name.
Porcelain fruit boxes float above tables,
sterling silver ice cream cone holders
twirl upside down on the cat's dozing head.

For years I developed radar against malls.
So what is it that secretly applauds
this army of catalogues marching upon my house?
I could be in the bosom of poverty, still they arrive.
I could be dead, picked apart by vultures,
still they would tell me
what socks to wear in my climbing boots.

Stay true, catalogues, protect me
from the wasteland where whimsy and impulse
never camp.
Be my companion on this journey between dusts,
between vacancy and that smiling stare
that is citizen of every climate
but customer to nothing,
even air.

What He Said to His Enemies

He could hear them off in the forest,
massive branches breaking:
you are no good, will never be any good.

Sometimes they followed him,
rubbing out his tracks.
They wanted him to get lost
in the world of trees,
stand silently forever, holding up his hands.

At night he watched
the streetlamp's light
soaking into his lawn.
He could bathe in its cool voice,
roll over to a whole different view.
What made them think
the world's room was so small?

On the table he laid out his clothes,
arranging the cuffs.
What he said to his enemies
was a window pushed high as it would go.
Come in, look for me where you think
I am. Then when you see no one is there,
we can talk.

NAOMI SHIHAB NYE was born in 1952 and grew up in St. Louis, Missouri; Jerusalem; and San Antonio, Texas, where she now lives with her husband, Michael, and their son, Madison. Her books of poems are *Different Ways to Pray*, *Hugging the Jukebox* (selected by Josephine Miles for the National Poetry Series), *Yellow Glove*, and *Red Suitcase*. The recipient of the Lavan Award from the Academy of American Poets, Nye is a frequent guest at schools, workshops, and conferences, and has journeyed to the Middle East and Asia on several speaking tours sponsored by Arts America/ U.S.I.A. In 1995 she appeared in the PBS series, "The Language of Life with Bill Moyers." She has also written and edited numerous books for young readers, including *Sitti's Secrets* (named a *School Library Journal* Best Book for 1994), *This Same Sky*, an award-winning anthology of international poetry, and *The Tree is Older Than You Are: A Bilingual Gathering of Poems and Stories from Mexico*.

The photographs on the front cover and the half title page are of Sitti Khadra, the author's Palestinian grandmother. They were taken in 1983 and 1992 by Michael Nye. Khadra Shihab lived in a small West Bank village. She died in 1994 at the age of 106.

Marcia Barrentine designed the cover of *Words Under the Words* with design assistance and digital production by Roberta Lampert. Tom Booth designed the book. The typeface is Janson Text. Thomson-Shore of Dexter, Michigan, printed the book on acid-free paper. *Words Under the Words* is the first title published by Far Corner Books of Portland, Oregon. ◼